MW00849947

"It took me back to those frightening days when I began ministering to soldiers in peace and the moments in combat when I felt exactly like the main character –powerless. I believe *A Chaplain's Battle* will become a cornerstone in ministry and caregiving."

— CHAPLAIN (COL) TERRY W. AUSTIN

"Chaplain Michael D. Jaques has touched the pulse of the combat chaplain in his book, *A Chaplain's Battle*. In a very practical and theologically insightful way, he takes his reader from the firefight to a confrontation with his own conscience... What good can a chaplain do in combat? Jaques explains what causes the doubts and fears with which a servant of God wrestles in combat and how they can make lasting peace with the haunting images they carry with them.

— CHAPLAIN JAMES A. RYAN, JR. (COL – RET), USA

A CHAPLAIN'S BATTLE

TRANSCENDING POWERLESSNESS IN AN EXPLOSIVE WORLD

MICHAEL D. JAQUES LTC, US ARMY

For my beautiful wife Cindy, and my amazing kids
Michael Jr. and Madison

TABLE OF CONTENTS

FIVE ESSENTIAL ATTAINMENTS FOR CAREGIVERS

PROLOGUE | UNSPOKEN

WE THINK OF THEM AS POWERFUL DEFENDERS OF LIFE. IN MOMENTS when bullets are flying, fires are blazing, blood is spurting, and significant tragedy is looming, they must make life-or-death decisions. Their instinct is always to save those men and women whose lives are threatened.

Sadly some of those die in their care. Others are maimed or emotionally disabled by their trauma. Afterward, our soldiers, police officers, clergy, paramedics, and firefighters often feel a powerlessness that most are unable or unwilling to admit. Shame, embarrassment, or a crushing sense of failure inhibit conversations with co-workers. Troubling "why" questions haunt their sleep. Many struggle to admit mistakes or weaknesses. These universal feelings cause dedicated men and women to think they should abandon their calling.

We dare not let that happen. Our society cannot afford to lose these compassionate and dedicated people. Our survival, in war or peace, depends on their willingness to serve. We all suffer if their ranks are diminished because they mistakenly believe they are inadequate or berate themselves when they cannot save the lives of the bereft, the stricken, or the innocent casualties of terrorism.

I came to this topic as an Army chaplain deployed several times to war zones during our nation's participation in the global war on terror. Through interviews and research, I quickly learned that this sense of powerlessness is widespread and unspoken. Yet when given the chance, I found my colleagues and other frontline caregivers quite willing to share their experiences—if only to help the thousands of other men and women who have yet to understand and overcome it.

Therapists, theologians, and researchers have known for decades that committed caregivers—those whose primary purpose in life is to assist others in crisis—all suffer from the debilitating experience of powerlessness.

Police officers feel it when they see innocent people suffer from criminal violence; doctors and nurses experience it when they can't save the lives of chronically ill children; and first responders struggle with it when they see lives torn apart in accidents and fires.

Even leaders whose responsibilities do not include administering healthcare or protective services may fall into despair if they make a mistake that they perceive as harming the people they have sworn to help.

The five attainments I humbly offer herein are an answer to this pervasive problem.

———

THESE SIMPLE YET PROFOUND steps to freedom are achieved by embracing an unexpected source of liberation—a willingness to accept our weakness. We cannot be broken by our human limitations if we are willing to recognize them. In accepting them, we open ourselves to the only power that can help us transcend the explosive, often inexplicable world we live and work in.

Caregivers take heart. Your gift to society does not need to spell personal ruin. Quite the opposite. Your commitment to shaking free of despair is a path to the fulfillment you imagined when you first answered the call.

To express the range of emotions and situations many caregivers experience, I created a fictional character, Chaplain Tim Parker. His traumas and challenges are based on real events that either my colleagues or I have experienced. This approach allows me to be a storyteller and a facilitator of dialogue about our true-life struggles. I believe these stories will help us embrace and ponder the extent of our unique role in the world.

Drawing on my research and interviews with other caregivers about powerlessness, I also offer analysis of the chaplain's travels. By blending a fictional narrative with the insights of modern and historic thought leaders, I present the paradox of faith in our unstable world.

Michael D. Jaques
Wounded Warrior Chaplain, US Army Reserve

1

RECEIVING THE WOUNDED

THE DAY RONNY DIED

CHAPLAIN TIM PARKER WATCHED AS THE C-17 GLOBEMASTER pierced the cloud layer and descended. After six years in the service, he was still in awe of how quickly Air National Guard troops could turn these giant cargo planes into flying intensive care units that shuttled wounded soldiers from our Ramstein airbase in Germany. It was an example of the strength and ingenuity of the military.

Capt. Parker, the crew-cut son of a Texas military family, was proud to be a member of the welcoming team. They watched the arrival of buses and medical vehicles parked outside the aeromedical staging facility at Joint Base Andrews near Washington, D.C.

As the enormous gray bird touched the ground, the chaplain exchanged greetings with others on his bus. Each branch of the military was represented by a liaison who would greet the plane along with doctors, nurses, and mental health experts. Together they would assist the arriving troops who would be taken to other destinations—Walter Reed, Fort Bragg, or an airbase in San Antonio. Some would be fed a meal and assigned overnight lodgings before moving on.

Usually, the chaplain enjoyed these events. He knew how

much it meant to injured troops to be greeted on home soil. Yet his initial pleasure at watching the plane arrive safely quickly surrendered to anxiety. He became so pensive he barely responded to the Army nurse who sat next to him.

"More passengers than usual, Chaplain," she said. Silence. Then he looked up and gave an uneasy nod. "It worries me."

He would have preferred to say nothing, but he did not want to seem rude.

"Me too. The war, it's still …"

She finished his sentence. "… messing up good people."

He nodded and whispered, "Yes."

During the early days of Operation Iraqi Freedom, there were as many as fifty passengers on the C-17s. That number had shrunk in recent years, sometimes to as few as five or ten. Yet this flight carried twenty-nine service members, and that was troubling. Parker had deployed several times to the Middle East. He had witnessed the carnage of war— multiple fatalities and injuries from improvised bombs, merciless mortar and rocket attacks, and enemy suicide missions. He also knew too well the troubles soldiers faced on the home front—missed birthdays and holidays, marital and financial problems, kids failing in school and unexpected deaths of friends or family members. Feelings of guilt, inadequacy, and helplessness compounded with the daily stress of trying to survive to see the next day.

On this day's flight, all the patients had life-altering issues to contend with. Many had been wounded in action and airlifted to Germany for intensive care. Among them were young men and a woman who had lost limbs, been paralyzed or were suffering from brain injuries. The chaplain was already anticipating the fear and questions that would be etched on their faces.

Other soldiers had suffered accidental injuries while fulfilling basic duties or recreating— broken bones for example. Civilians stateside might assume these troops felt lucky to be shipped home without life-threatening wounds. Tim Parker knew otherwise: Most felt guilty about leaving their fellow warriors; men and women who faced death every day.

Dire medical diagnoses also brought troops home. One Michigander had learned that he had terminal cancer, and a female G.I. was emotionally wounded by a sexual assault.

The chaplain knew their stories because each time a C-17 landed, he was given a list with short profiles of each passenger. He stared now at one name and injury synopsis as his vehicle began to move forward.

"Here we go," the Army nurse said.

This time the chaplain did not respond. Not even a nod. Instead, he stared out the window, overcome with nausea and enough tension to make breathing difficult. The discomfort increased as the huge aircraft taxied to a stop.

Greeting this arrival would be different from all the others. He would board the plane burdened by an event that jabbed his conscience whenever it came to mind. The knives of regret would be ever sharper now when he came face-to-face with the man who had witnessed his moment of shame. The chaplain was sure he would be recognized by the soldier who had since risen to the rank of sergeant.

"Chaplain?"

He startled when he felt the nurse touch his arm. "Huh?"

"Are you OK?"

"Oh, sorry, yes. Yes, I'm fine," he lied.

———

THE ROCKET ATTACK began at midday, and like all the other enemy onslaughts, it came without warning or mercy. It was 2004, the chaplain's first deployment, and he had dozed off in his tent on an Army base near Fallujah. The first screams he heard were the rockets speeding overhead, shredding the peace of a sunny day, then exploding helter-skelter in various sectors of the camp.

When he jolted upright, the Bible that had been spread open on his chest fell heavily to the floor. As Capt. Parker leaped to his feet, he landed awkwardly on the Good Book. Before he could stand, he was hurled backward by a blast that shook the ground like a violent earthquake. Alone in his barracks, he heard for the first time the terrible agony of shocked human beings crying out for help. At first, he froze, paralyzed by fear. Next, he willed himself to run toward the horror.

A mortar round had blown apart a tent where troops slept. Some would never again awaken to the joy of a new day and a fresh cup of coffee. Some who survived had been ripped open. They howled and cursed as blood spurted from their wounds. A few others, miraculously, stumbled out of the flames with burns, bloodied faces, or broken bones.

Parker joined other young men and women in fatigue pants and T-shirts who rushed toward the carnage, shouting, cursing, even bawling at the sight of fallen friends. Above the fray, mortar fire continued to hiss and intimidate. The chaplain felt relieved that his arms and legs were still functioning despite the panic and chaos. He and other personnel picked up the wounded and rushed them to a makeshift triage area. Back and forth, again and again, he helped deliver ravaged bodies, explosions unyielding.

Yet the weight of the falling sky and mounting casualties took its toll. He was a man of God, his mere presence invoked a higher power. In a moment of unfathomable despair, surrounded by corpses and dismembered beings, he felt useless and even betrayed. *Why am I here? What called me to this place?*

Then a hand gripped his combat boot and would not let go. The chaplain looked down at a man whose torso had been ripped open. Guts spilled out like lava and stained the earth a dark red.

"Save me," he whispered. "I don't want to die. *Please, Chaplain.*"

Although the chaplain was dressed like the other troops, his

T-shirt included a black cross over his heart. It was his duty to assist and pray for anyone who needed him. But he stood mute, unable to move as he stared down at the mangled soldier whose eyes pleaded for assurances, comfort, or maybe a prayer.

"Please, Chaplain. Please?" "Help him, damn it!"

Stunned, Parker turned to find a soldier who raged and glared at him in disbelief. Then he watched as the G.I. fell to his knees to cradle his friend's head.

"Hang in there, Ronny, OK? The doc will be here soon. You're going to be fine."

The wounded man began to sob. "I can't, Matt. I'm dying. I can feel it."

"No, no. The chaplain is here, and he's ..."

Numb, trembling, Parker felt like he would implode into grains of sand. He was no longer threatened by the mortar attack. A sense of powerlessness had eviscerated him.

Then the raging soldier, Pvt. Matt Kennedy, shot up from the ground, grabbed the chaplain and shook him so hard the man of God thought his neck might snap.

"You're useless, preacher! This man is dying. Say something! Bless him! At least bless him, damn it!"

Blood had dried in the corners of the injured man's mouth, and his chest had stopped rising.

It took four infantrymen to pull Pvt. Kennedy away from the chaplain, who stood for a long time in triage, shaken and ashamed.

When the rockets finally stopped, and relative calm returned to the base, the chaplain found a remote spot, fell to his knees, and tilted his eyes to the darkening sky.

"Dear Lord, why would you bring me here, but not give me the power to save lives and heal?"

———

As the chaplain walked up the ramp at the back of the C-17, he immediately saw the most critically wounded troops. They were always the first removed from the aircraft, stretched out on hospital beds installed on each side of the otherwise raw interior. An Air National Guard crew could transform a plane this size into a trauma center in about ninety minutes including modern medical equipment that monitored each patient's condition.

As flight physicians and nurses prepared for the transfer, Capt. Parker greeted each warrior.

"How are you doing? How was the flight? They feed you well?"

Some smiled, pleased with the light humor and a handshake. Others were unresponsive because of induced sleep or their fragile conditions. A couple expressed fear for the future, fully knowing their travails were far from over.

"I'm scared, Chaplain," one said.

"We've got you covered. You're home now. Rest easy."

"But ..."

The chaplain didn't rush. He answered questions as well as he could and murmured prayers with the intention of connecting with each of the twenty-nine passengers. Immersed in the goodwill of welcoming personnel, he was at ease.

The anxiety returned when Parker walked into the section of the plane where troops who did not need immediate medical attention were waiting to disembark. Sgt. Matt Kennedy would be here.

He was easy to spot. His broad back and height distinguished him as a superior warrior. Yet his physical strength masked a contradiction. His injury synopsis said he'd been evacuated after threatening suicide.

The chaplain knew he could not avoid the reunion, so he moved forward, prepared to meet his fate.

"Welcome home, Sgt. Kennedy," he said, reaching out his hand. "Remember me?" The recognition was immediate, if not exactly warm.

"Chaplain." Kennedy paused, nodding slightly as he took in a deep breath. "Fallujah. The day Ronny died."

"Tough day."

"Yeah. For all of us, right?" Kennedy averted his eyes, as though he needed a moment to recover from the reminder of a terrible loss. "But you know what? You gave me a lot that day."

The chaplain couldn't help but search for sarcasm, or a subtle slight of some kind. He found no such thing in Kennedy's voice or demeanor.

"Forgive me, but are you sure you remember who I am?"

"Oh, yeah."

"OK. But then how was it that I helped you? I did nothing. I watched your friend die. And I've been …"

"Beating yourself up ever since, right Chaplain?"

Now the chaplain paused and reminded himself to breathe. "It's a painful memory."

The two men stood awkwardly, each over six-feet tall, as members of the welcoming team began to guide the men and women to their next destinations.

Finally, Kennedy spoke. "Look, they've threatened to serve us a meal before we're all shipped out. I hope it's not something they pour out of a can. I'm tired of MRE's. Remember those?"

"Meals ready to eat."

"So they say."

The chaplain laughed. Camaraderie, shared experience, a salve for so many wounds. "Anyway, can we talk in the cafeteria while I stuff my face?"

"I'd like that."

Parker resumed his duties, chatted with the other soldiers, and then heard Kennedy call from a distance.

"Chaplain, there was nothing you could have done for Ronny."

He believed Kennedy was only trying to absolve him of blame. Even so, the chaplain felt his heart sink—again.

2

SUICIDE MISSION

"THERE WAS NOTHING YOU COULD HAVE DONE."

THE CHAPLAIN KNEW SGT. KENNEDY'S STATEMENT WAS ONLY PARTLY true. He could have done something. He could have knelt and comforted the dying soldier. He could have held his hand, given him assurances about the hereafter, or promised to contact his family. Had he done that much, he might have been able to expunge the unsettling memory.

Yet there was more to his distress than the Fallujah tragedy. Before his first deployment, the chaplain brimmed with his own virtue. He was sure he would bring meaningful insights and support to American troops in combat. That naïve confidence had vanished within days of his arrival in Iraq.

The troops he encountered suffered from a plethora of emotional issues—bereavement, despair, identity crisis, damaged relationships—and they weren't always receptive to God's Word or practical suggestions that might ease their pain. They wanted an immediate resolution of their psychological stress, yet their demands felt far beyond his capabilities.

When Ronny was dying and pleaded, *"Save me,"* Tim Parker lost all objectivity. He thought he was expected to miraculously heal the soldier's ravaged body rather than soothe the man's soul.

And just like Sgt. Kennedy had said, he'd spent a year beating himself up over that failure. During that time, he knew he needed to do an honest self-evaluation with his supervisor.

That's what caregivers are supposed to do, but it was too painful. So he waited until he got back to the States to seek help.

Capt. Parker might have quit his ministry were it not for the mentor he met upon his return. He was flattered when Garrison Chaplain Robert Brand invited him to meet for coffee in his office. Patiently, the man with graying temples and the silver eagle of a full colonel on his uniform asked gentle questions about the war and its effect on the chaplain.

"How are you feeling? Are you OK?"

"Yes, Sir. Thank you for asking. I'm fine."

"Mm-hm. You sleep well and—?"

"Oh, yes," the chaplain insisted, stubbornly pretending he was impervious to trauma and consequence.

Colonel Brand nodded kindly, then probed more deeply. He asked about burial rights for the fallen troops, how it felt to minister those services, and other facts of life on an Army base in a foreign country. As the interview continued, the younger chaplain felt pressed for answers and realized he was being led into deep waters. Before he could pull free and race back to the shallows, a wave of emotion rose from within. Bawling shook his body so violently that he felt like he would shatter. Amid the flood of tears, he felt an embrace and heard a voice.

"Son, we have to accept our limitations, or they will tear us apart. Let God work through you. And accept whatever outcome He provides. *That's an order.*"

The firmness in the command caused the young chaplain to clear his eyes. He was relieved to see that Brand was smiling.

"But I … I feel so . . ."

Col. Brand finished his sentence. "Powerless?"

The younger man nodded, and the tears began to flow again.

"Sooner or later, we all face that enemy. Happened to me, too.

And I'll admit that to this day, sometimes I still feel it creeping back into my consciousness. Know what I say then?"

"No, Sir."

"I say, 'Get lost.'" Both men smiled.

"Why don't you come back tomorrow, Tim? I want to hear about your wife and daughter. And we'll talk more about the condition many good people hate to name. Sound good?"

———

THE CHAPLAIN FOUND Sgt. Kennedy in a dining hall that resounded with friendly voices, clattering plates, and shuffling boots. He joined him and smiled as he watched the soldier devouring the roast beef and noodles piled high on his plate. When Sgt. Kennedy's plate was nearly clean, he asked his question.

"On the plane, you spoke about the day we lost Ronny. You said I'd given you a lot. How could that possibly be true?"

Moving beef gravy and noodles around his plate, Kennedy was not quick to answer.

"Not that it didn't take me a while, chaplain. You might not remember, but I was shipped out of there right after that attack. Otherwise, they might have thrown me in the stockade for my..." He stopped eating and faced Parker. "I apologize for how I treated you."

The chaplain shrugged. "No problem, I get it."

"Thank you. Anyway, I guess they needed every soldier they had, so I was disciplined, but you know, minor stuff. I ended up in Afghanistan, and that's when I realized, and this may sounds funny. . . "

"What?"

"I realized when you couldn't move or react, that you're no different than me. Just because you were a chaplain didn't mean you could move mountains."

"Oh, I disagree."

That sparked a laugh and eased whatever tension remained between them. Kennedy sat back smiling and wiped his mouth with a napkin.

"You couldn't stop the enemy from wanting to kill us. You carried a Bible, not a bazooka."

"Well, obviously, all that is true. But, sergeant . . ."

"Call me Matt."

"OK. Thank you. Matt, I still don't get it. How was it that I *helped* you?"

"I realized I could make my own decisions. I had kind of looked at our commanding officers, and even chaplains, as father figures. Like if something goes wrong, they'll fix it. But rank isn't a higher power, is it? Hopefully, it's earned, but Jesus . . . Oh, sorry, I didn't mean to name-drop."

"I understand."

"Well, then, seeing you standing there—and, hey, you grabbed bodies out of the fire, you were involved—but seeing you freeze up really pissed me off. At first. Then months later, after reviewing my own long lists of failures, I was grateful. I thought, *no more false gods*. No more thinking somebody is better than me or can do something I'm not capable of doing myself. Not sure any of this is making sense."

Kennedy went back to his food while Parker pondered what had been shared. It did make sense, in some ways. But it raised some tough questions, too. Did it mean the soldier had lost faith or had no god he might call upon?

And then there was the troubling matter of why Sgt. Matt Kennedy had been sent home.

"Need some dessert, Matt?"

"Oh, yes. But not before I get another plate of this beefy noodle thing. Not bad."

As Matt returned to their table with another full plate, the chaplain reached into his breast pocket and pulled out the list of soldiers he'd been reviewing when the C-17 landed. He spread it on the dining table. Matt didn't miss a beat.

"Is that my report card, chaplain?"

"Yes, in a way. Mind if I ask about it?"

"Suicide."

"Right."

"You're wondering . . ."

"Lots of things." But it was not the chaplain's style to be confrontational.

"You know how it works."

"What? The Army?"

"Maybe in some situations, suicide is a rational choice."

The chaplain recoiled. This was a belief he could not condone. Now he truly believed his inaction in Iraq had harmed this soldier.

"*Chill*, Chaplain. I'm OK."

"So you're *not* mentally unstable?"

"Whoa."

"What?"

Sgt. Kennedy lowered his voice and looked around the dining room. "We're just talking, right? Off the record?"

"I just want to know you're OK, Matt."

The sergeant gulped ice water from a tall glass, then leaned forward.

"I faked it. The suicide thing. I'd finally had enough. My wife wants a divorce, and we have two kids. Commander wouldn't approve a home visit. He said stay and fight. And that's the problem. For years, I've been fighting for my country, but not for my own family. And I'm blaming me, not anybody else, because I haven't been committed to my wife and kids, not really. I'm tight with my tribe overseas. Infantry. And I hate being away from them, but dammit, I never had a chance to bond with my own kids."

The chaplain was moved by Kennedy's plight because he had been deployed to Iraq for the first time when his daughter was barely a year old. When he returned home, his little girl did not know who her father was.

Chaplains tried but often failed to persuade commanding officers to allow soldiers to return home for family matters. In desperation, some soldiers whose requests were denied played the suicide card. It didn't often work, so Matt must have been very convincing. That hurt. After risking death, a brave soldier was forced to lie. Invariably, he would face another kind of harm — the moral damage that occurs when we betray what we know is true and right.

"You're in my tribe, too, Chaplain. You know that I hope. We shared something important over there. And here, too. Thanks for listening."

"I'll pray for your family."

"My wife is gone. She's in another man's bed now. But I've got to hug my kids again and ask, '*Who's your daddy?*' I hope they know the answer."

The chaplain winced at the sight of such pain in this father's eyes. As the tanned, muscular soldier stood, Tim Parker could think of nothing better to offer than a recitation, which he whispered:

"No one who has sacrificed home, spouse, brothers and sisters, parents, children or whatever will lose out. It will all come back multiplied many times over in your lifetime. And then the bonus of eternal life."

"Who said that?"

"Jesus Christ."

Nodding, then, "Got to catch a plane to San Antonio."

"What about pie and coffee?"

He grinned. "Very tempting, but . . ."

"God bless you, Matt."

Sgt. Kennedy stopped and squared his body. "If there is a God."

"And if there is not?"

The wounded warrior bit his lip as his eyes took on water. "Somehow I'm still here. And so are you. Maybe that's a sign."

The chaplain watched Sgt. Matt Kennedy exit the dining

facility. He assumed he would never again see this particular member of his tribe.

Something else stirred in him, a feeling of being more secure and skilled in his calling than ever before. This chance reunion with Matt Kennedy was a gift—one that freed him from a

crippling past. It reminded him that it was not within his rank, pay grade, or personal power to control a soldier's feelings and beliefs. Perhaps he had achieved what Col. Brand called the First Attainment.

3

THE FIRST ATTAINMENT

"I AM POWERLESS."

BY NOT ACCEPTING POWERLESSNESS, CAREGIVERS BEGIN TO DEVALUE their contributions to society—their Army division, city, or niche community. Parker expressed that frustrating digression the next time he met with Col. Brand and opened up about the rocket attack in Iraq.

"I'm at the aid station, and casualties are screaming out in pain. Yet I couldn't help. Not even the soldier who begged me."

Brand gave him a stern look. "You couldn't hold his hand, talk, and pray with him?"

"It seemed useless."

"Why?"

"Yes, why? If we can't stop death, if we can't stop all the killing … why bother praying?"

"To bear witness."

"What do you mean?"

"Just listening is a service," Brand said. "That soldier desperately needed to be seen and heard and understood in his time of need. He wasn't blaming you for his condition. Show an interest, engage the person in trauma. The simplest things we can offer get lost when we're in a crisis."

"I didn't want to just listen. I wanted to fix things, make him better. I wanted to . . ."

"*Save* him. But that's not your job."

————

THE ARMY IS LARGELY MADE up of people who focus on solving problems. Mostly, they are doers and fixers. When soldiers are given orders to deploy and fight the nation's wars, completing the mission is their primary focus. They make plans, coordinate efforts, overcome obstacles, and make personal sacrifices so they can say, 'Mission accomplished.'

Many clergy persons who minister to these doers and fixers are cut from the same cloth.

They have equal determination to care for and minister to these soldiers. Army chaplains, sometimes by default, are given a wide range of ministerial responsibilities. In addition to providing worship services, they are counselors, advocates, and problem solvers for the soldiers. Often, soldiers come to them when their perceived options have run out.

Unfortunately, while on deployment, soldiers experience problems that neither they nor their leaders can solve. This inability to fix the problem, by people who are by nature fixers, creates a sense of powerlessness for all involved. For example, when soldiers receive 'Dear John' letters or hear of significant medical or financial issues at home or of the deaths of extended family members, they typically want to hop the first flight home. While leadership may sympathize with their circumstances, they may not be able to authorize a home visit. And chaplains may not be able to comfort the distressed soldiers. Therefore, all these fixers experience feelings of powerlessness.

In interviews for this book, chaplains admitted they often felt powerless to help soldiers solve fundamental problems during deployments. While issues they face might seem unique to chaplains serving overseas, clergy, therapists, and counselors at home suffer similar frustrations.

When counseling a grieving person, the therapist knows the person needs time to process and heal, but they are pressed for immediate fixes. In times of crisis, both counselors and clients grasp for any kind of solution, even one they might not believe to be effective. Ultimately, those who come to chaplains for help may leave as frustrated as when they walked in.

Lack of objectivity also plays a role. In some cases, inexperienced chaplains and other caregivers try to fix the other person's problem because they see it as a challenge to be won or they empathize so intensely they take ownership of the issue. When they can't bring immediate resolution, these caregivers begin to feel like they have failed, like they have not measured up to expectations. The chaplains interviewed described those negative feelings this way:

- "My failure made me feel inferior."
- "I feel guilty and a huge sense of inadequacy."
- "I must not be doing what I'm supposed to be doing with my life."
- "I prayed for safety, but safety didn't come. Soldiers still died."

Isolation is another consequence of powerlessness. Often caregivers withdraw, which renders them even less effective. One said, "It's like I built a wall. I feel isolated from my job." Another said, "Except for contact with my mentors, I feel alone. Like I'm on an island." Several expressed a desire to leave, saying they no longer recognized that God has a purpose for them.

These feelings of inadequacy and isolation strike at the core of their faith and identity.

- One chaplain said, "What I've experienced here has

made me doubt my faith and where I'm at in my calling."

- Another veteran caregiver said, "When I think about giving up, it sends me into a dark place that I can't pull myself out of."
- "The sense of isolation and powerlessness has made me want to leave because I no longer recognize God's purpose for me here."

To be sure, caregivers get shaken by what they experience during a crisis. The feelings of powerlessness may raise personal doubts about their beliefs. But as Col. Brand counseled, the first step of overcoming—or attainment as he called it—is to accept powerlessness as part of the job.

Parker's successful meeting with Sgt. Kennedy didn't change the facts of what happened in Fallujah. And it didn't alter Kennedy's skepticism about God. The chaplain had to recognize that. What transformed him in that encounter was the ability to see and accept the powerlessness of his circumstances.

Paul the Apostle wrote, "But He said to me, 'My grace is sufficient for you, for My power is made perfect in weakness.' Therefore I will boast all the more gladly about My weaknesses, so that Christ's power may rest on Me," (2 Cor. 12:9, NIV).

This paradoxical idea of strength through weakness is one of the major themes throughout the Bible. Beginning with Abraham and continuing through the climactic example of Jesus, God has used people, who acknowledged their weaknesses and depended on the Divine, to make them strong through their shortcomings.

Today we are still coming to terms with Paul's statement from two millennia ago. In one study, researchers asked nurses how they made sense of their powerlessness in easing the suffering of children in neonatal intensive care units (NICU). Like characters in the Bible, the nurses recognized their weaknesses and attributed the meaning of the anguish to a cosmic or divine plan.

In a sense, God leaves people to their suffering as Jesus was abandoned to His travail.

Yet the caregiver becomes a visible representation of whatever higher power is meaningful to the person in pain.

The representation experience happens most often when something goes terribly wrong, in war or at home. The soldier in crisis notices the cross on a uniform. He says, "Hey, there's a chaplain here." Notice the soldier did not say, "Hey, God has arrived." No, merely His representative. That alone can be a great comfort in a time of crisis.

If you are called upon to help another soul in crisis, hold in mind the nurse in NICU, the battlefield medic, the police officer, or the many others like Capt. Parker who know they can't fix everything. Sometimes they feel like they can't fix *anything*. They have reached The First Attainment of Caregivers—accepting powerlessness.

4

THE POWERLESS MANTRA

REPEATING SIMPLE TRUTHS

THE AMBUSH NEAR FALLUJAH HIT THEM AS SWIFTLY AS A TRAIN slamming into a stranded car. The loud and disorienting collision of forces sent the Army night patrol scrambling for whatever cover they could find on a rocky hill. Lt. Carey Suarez watched in horror as enemy fire took down his two-point men like wheat stalks cut by a scythe. There was nothing he could do to save them, so he turned to regroup his other men.

Shouting orders under a crescent moon, the lieutenant quickly executed a strategy that would send some men into retreat, while others repositioned, trying to outflank the opposition.

Lt. Suarez also defended against an angry thought that refused to surrender: *This should not have happened.* He had worked for two years with Capt. Daniel Roth, a trusted battalion intelligence officer who had guided them on many successful reconnaissance missions. His grasp of the physical terrain as well as his understanding of the population—friends and enemies— was second to none. But the intel officer was away on leave and apparently hadn't been in on the planning for this mission.

"Lieutenant! They're coming around. Drop back. We have to drop back!"

The corporal was right. Suarez immediately saw a swarm of shadows, muzzles blazing, move toward the already fragile American stakeout.

"Move left. Down the gully!" The Lieutenant's shouted order sent his men sprinting down the descending path toward a rocky outcrop where they hoped to fend off the assault.

"Move, move, move!"

The soldier who had first noticed the attackers raced past Suarez, who savagely fired his weapon, holding ground until the others could run to safety.

Not everyone was fast enough. Two more infantry members cried out after being riddled with bullets. The enemy, pressing its advantage, began hurling grenades.

As his men hunkered down behind him, the Lieutenant flashed on a scary moment he experienced as a boy when he had nearly drowned. He was swimming alone in the Pacific Ocean when a riptide yanked him far away from shore. That's what this attack felt like. He was in the grip of an enemy force that seemed to grow larger and deadlier as it closed in.

Yet here were his men again, rushing toward him from behind, throwing fire so he could escape.

"Move, Lieutenant. Now!"

In unison, his infantrymen unleashed a barrage of munitions that lit the narrow passage with a torrent of red flame.

Suarez jumped up from a squat and bolted toward his unit's position. This too felt like that awful boyhood experience, when somehow he had wrestled free of the riptide and swam to shore exhausted.

As he hustled, he saw the faces of his saviors as they waged war on his behalf. His heart leaped. He would live. He would survive another hazardous episode so he could insist to the commanders, *This should not have happened.*

Then his head snapped forward, and his neck exploded in searing pain. As his body collapsed from an enemy bullet, he could not fathom how or why the tide that was taking him away had turned red.

———

Capt. Parker had been speaking with Daniel Roth for nearly an hour, but their conversation was going nowhere. Like a runner on an oval track, the intelligence officer would not move away from his crippling guilt; he kept circling back. Unsure of how to relieve Roth of his misery, the chaplain began another lap by repeating simple truths, things they had already discussed.

"You were sent away from the base for some time off. Regulations. You didn't ask for it. In fact, you were long overdue."

Since the beginning of the Global War on Terror (GWOT), active duty soldiers had been deploying to Iraq or Afghanistan as often as every other year. At first, the deployments lasted one year. Rest and Recuperation (R&R) leave was authorized near the midpoint of the tour. Later, deployments were shortened to nine months, and R&R was eliminated.

"It doesn't matter," Roth insisted. "It's my fault."

The ambush that killed Lt. Carey Suarez had caused five other casualties. Before presiding over their funeral on base, the chaplain had a much more difficult task. The survivors of the disastrous patrol couldn't sleep. The chaplain had been summoned in the wee hours to minister to the group. The men asked endless questions, most of which began and ended with an agonizing *why*. It was evident that Suarez was a man who was not only respected, but loved and admired for his leadership. When the questions ceased, Parker asked them to kneel, and he led them in prayer.

The next day during the funeral ceremony, the chaplain spotted a lone figure standing apart from the crowd of mourners. He didn't know it was Capt. Roth until two weeks later when the battalion commander asked for an intervention, of sorts.

"Explain to me how it is your fault," the chaplain went on.

"We've already talked about this."

"I know, but . . ."

"And don't give me all that religious bunk, either. It won't help anything."

When speaking with the soldiers after the ambush, it had been the non-believers, the agnostics, and atheists, who had been inconsolable. They had no context for understanding or accepting death. Whereas the other soldiers of various faiths, though equally upset, began turning to their faith for support, even though there were no immediate answers for why things had gone awry.

"I understand, Daniel. But the commander has asked me to . . ."

"He doesn't get it, and he never will!"

The chaplain remained silent. The more he pressed, the less cooperative Roth became. The well-liked and talented battalion intel officer had become a riddle to everyone around him, particularly to the commander who was tough and temperamental. He had made it clear to the chaplain that Roth must resume his duties immediately. No wonder, then, that Parker had been hasty in his first attempt to ignite the soldier's sense of responsibility. Only now had he come to suspect he had misread Roth. The man was grieving, more so than the others. Yet his reluctance to engage seemed to suggest a secret, something Roth was guarding behind a wall he had carefully erected.

"Just—if you would, please—tell me what you would have done differently. From a tactical point of view."

"I never should have left. I've told you that."

"No, I mean . . ."

"The planning for that mission should not have happened without me. I knew it might be in play, but I didn't think they'd move on it so soon."

"Maybe they had to."

"If they trust my skills so much, why did they rush?"

"Again, you had no control over the timetable or . . ."

"Chaplain, I realize you're on a mission."

"Sorry?"

"The commander. You're his last hope, right?"

"Daniel, my question was … please … all I want to know is how would you have planned the Suarez mission differently."

The chaplain had no real strategy in mind. All he wanted was to avoid the circuitous wrangling that had turned Roth into an adversary. The man's keen intelligence was apparent from the start; his mind was a multi-layered, three-dimensional strategic map that seemed to morph at will—a defense mechanism of considerable sophistication.

Yet the chaplain had noticed that the name itself—Suarez— had caused a different reaction than general questions about the mission. *Listen, simply listen*, he told himself, remembering the lessons Col. Brand had instilled in him before this deployment, his second.

"Look … I don't know why, but I have a feel for the land-scape, for the culture here. It's intuitive, things come to me, and I've come to trust my instincts. Lt. Suarez got that. He'd come to me to brainstorm, to jam like we were musicians. We'd go through protocols; we'd envision scenarios beyond the grasp of mere data, and then we'd create a plan that sometimes confounded the commander. Eventually, even old Block Head came to realize that what we'd created was … unique and viable."

The chaplain envied this ability to collaborate with another "player" on matters of such significance. So often the clergyman had felt solitary in his studies and journey as a caregiver.

"But you didn't always get to work together, did you?"

"No, but our success … the promising nature of our work … we became kind of superstitious."

"You had a bond."

Roth hesitated. "Yes."

"And obeying the order for a little R and R…"

"I was at rest *here*. It was weird because suddenly I didn't give a damn about a vacation. I could only relax when I was working through a confluence of complexities here with Carey."

The avalanche of loss fell on Roth so entirely the chaplain feared the officer would not recover. His demeanor, his bearing, seemed fragile as glass.

"I could have prevented those deaths, Chaplain. I'm sure of it. They'd all still be here, Carey and the other men."

"You don't know that."

"We had an understanding."

"You and Lt. Suarez."

"Yes."

"Of course. You were good together."

"We were close."

"Great friends."

"Yes, but … *more*."

One word brought down the barrier the chaplain had sensed earlier. *More.* Now he understood Roth's torment. These two dedicated men were lovers. Yet the *Don't Ask, Don't Tell* policy at the time demanded that they hide their feelings for fear of being disgraced and discharged without honors.

The revelation was not the only surprise. The chaplain also realized that Roth was suffering from the same powerlessness that had paralyzed him at Fallujah during his first deployment. He had been wrong to assume that only official caregivers were vulnerable to the curse. Roth's rank or title did not officially describe caregiver, but that's how he felt about his intelligence-gathering responsibilities.

The chaplain sat quietly for a long moment. Then he slipped off his chair onto his knees and shared the first attainment Col. Brand had taught him.

"I am powerless."

"What?" Roth stared at him, curious, confused.

"Say it with me, Daniel."

"Say what?"

"I am powerless."

"No!"

"OK. Then say, 'I Daniel Roth am God. I am omniscient and omnipresent.'"

"Well, that sure as hell isn't true." The chaplain nodded, smiled.

"Then let's head in the other direction. Say it with me. Please. I am ..."

"... Powerless."

The chaplain repeated the three words and soon Roth, pale, shoulders sagging, joined in and continued the mantra in a soft, exhausted voice. In a few minutes, Capt. Roth stood and walked out of the room, still lost in space.

5

THE SECOND ATTAINMENT

"I am *not* God."

THAT AWFUL FEELING OF POWERLESSNESS OFTEN STIRS UP A LONGING for power within caregivers. A recurring thought asserts, *"If only" I had the power, I could set things right.* Some caregivers deepen their agony by trying to take control. With a little success, a caregiver begins to think *I am God.*

No, you're not.

The impulse is understandable when in crisis, even if the overreach is seriously ironic. Chaplains know they need to trust God, but they may reach for anything but God to carry out their will and correct a problem. This same urge drives other caregivers, including parents and teachers.

In an interview, one chaplain articulated this struggle when he admitted, "We give ourselves glory when we get it right and exaggerate our view of ourselves too easily."

Yes, chaplains tend to feel pride when they can resolve an issue for a soldier. They feel powerless when they cannot. Unfortunately, pride and a lust for power tarnish the excellent intentions of merely wanting to help.

One Army chaplain said, "These 'I Am God' impulses remind me of an old commercial where the actor says, 'I'm not a doctor, but I play one on TV.' The inside joke among chaplains is, 'I'm not a god, but I play one as a chaplain.'"

Still yet another Army chaplain suggested the desire to be all-powerful may be a skewed form of asking for God's assistance and then expecting to feel the sensation of His empowerment. He labeled it the Inflatable Chaplain Syndrome.

But this brave clergyman went further by speaking of a troubling paradox. "When we think we can provide a positive resolution without God we are experiencing a lack of faith. At that moment, we don't believe He can and will deliver a profoundly satisfying outcome."

Army chaplains are trained in a culture that takes pride in its impressive firepower, air power, naval power, and brain power. Military men and women are taught to fix things, beat impossible odds, and win the day. So when chaplains cannot make a problem go away, they feel an innate sense of powerlessness and a greater desire to make something happen than a typical pastor.

In the previous story, Capt. Daniel Roth was starring in his own episode of "I am God." He was certain *he* could have prevented the ambush that killed his friend and lover. Chaplain Parker struggled with his own "I am God" issue when he went to his commander to appeal on Roth's behalf.

He suggested to the battalion commander that Roth was suicidal, and it was dangerous to expect Roth to resume his duties. He knew but couldn't say why Roth was so profoundly affected by this terrible loss of life.

"I believe Officer Roth should be allowed to go home," he pleaded.

"He's already had R & R!" the commander bellowed.

"He needs special care."

"He needs a kick in the ass."

"He's suffered a loss that. . ." The chaplain stopped short of outing Roth and Suarez.

How could he explain that death-in-the-family considerations might pertain? One thing he knew for sure: It was pointless to try to explain Roth's "I am God" vulnerabilities.

"This is war, chaplain. We eat loss for breakfast. If I go soft on one guy, I've got to bend to everybody else around here."

"That's not true, Sir."

"Say what?"

The chaplain's voice rose. "This is an isolated case that demands … "

"It's not going to happen, chaplain! And the next time you come in here spouting your gospel, you'd better be standing in the position of *attention*! Is that understood?"

Crushed by his inability to prevail, the chaplain left muttering about what he would do if only he were in charge. He experienced his very own "I am God" moment, though on a smaller stage than Roth's.

———

ONE OF THE most respected authorities on this subject is the late professor and theologian Charles V. Gerkin of Emory University. He fine-tuned his pastoral care theories over a thirty- year career as a pastor, professor, and author. His *Introduction to Pastoral Care* and other books and articles have influenced generations of pastors and chaplains.

Gerkin's works often examined the issue of powerlessness. He believed it was important for all human beings to have an accurate understanding of their power. In his opinion, the ability to understand the dynamics of personal power is twofold:

1. Learning how to comprehend and use the unique power within themselves as it relates to others.

2. Accepting the existential limits of their power.

In other words, people have power, and they also have limits to that authority. While people such as the battalion commander can exercise a great deal of force, even they will eventually experience feelings of powerlessness. And there is a considerable price to pay for those who refuse to understand this law of human nature.

Gerkin said those who do not accept the limitations of human power will be broken by those limitations. He taught that mature persons must realize their power, accept their powerlessness, and commit themselves to a higher power.

The distinction and relevance of pastoral care, according to Gerkin, are evidenced by God's providential care and the incarnation of Christ. A pastor can learn great insights and skills, but after all is said or done, he is still dependent on God. Pastors merely participate in what God is already doing.

At the core of this methodology is the ability of the caregiver to engage the person they are trying to help. Starting a dialogue that includes religious or general stories can reveal the actual cause of a crisis. Such engagement also takes the focus off the caregiver's sense of personal power. When inclined to think they have all the answers, a new thought emerges.

You're not God. Listen more, discuss more, then listen some more.

Caregivers often face the same problem as those they seek to counsel and serve— moments of doubt about God's providential care. This affects how they respond to death, despair, identity crises, and broken relationships. Therefore, restoring belief in the Divine is an integral part of vanquishing the debilitating God complex. Once that happens, Gerkin presents three steps that help caregivers return to their duties.

First, pastors must develop a healthy view of themselves as the physical representation of the power of God. During a crisis, God may seem absent or unreachable, but He is always present even though unseen. He never promised us a life without suffering, but He did promise to be *with us* in affliction. Therefore, in times of crisis, pastors are to be living symbols of the Divine—whatever that may mean for caregivers of different faiths.

Next, he suggests pastors must stand firm in the hope that God will intervene. The intent is to restore faith in the person who needs help. Sometimes, even people who profess faith forget they have resources beyond their own abilities to cope.

Finally, Professor Gerkin encouraged caregivers to become shepherds who help people work through a crisis that may be transformative, an instigator of change because this is how God works in the world. In this way, chaplains and counselors of all kinds are not simply observers. They become vital participants.

I am God.

No, you're not.

Yet as a caregiver you can become a facilitator, a virtual conduit, through whom a higher power may express His ability to form new realities.

Following the battalion commander's smackdown, Tim Parker soon arranged an overseas Skype conversation. Col. Brand could see the younger man was struggling again, but this time with a queasy mixture of feelings.

"I admit that I'm powerless, Sir."

"But?"

Tim Parker smiled at his mentor who, relaxed and friendly, stared out from the laptop screen.

"You never let me off the hook, do you, Sir?"

"What good would it do? Kindness is no kindness in that circumstance." Brand's reply had a calming effect. The truth may hurt, but it is also nourishing.

"But," the chaplain continued, "everywhere I look I see people with 'I am God' issues. I thought I was the only one with that problem."

The laughter from stateside lifted Parker's burden. Soon he was laughing too, overcome with the absurdity and foolishness of believing he was anything but human.

"My, oh my. It's true. Everybody and anybody who is willing to help another person can fall victim to these things. Intel officers, by-the-book commanders, parents, siblings, lovers ... the list never ends. But . . ."

"Yes?"

"Isn't it amazing that God gives us permission to take action even while accepting our limitations? If we only do that much, my goodness, we'll learn so much more about ourselves and the people we're trying to assist. Yes, everything from existential, ethical, and lifestyle issues that might be at the root of the crisis —their story—and then something more, something so sweet."

"What's that?"

"Being open to the possibility of grace."

6

LIFE AND DEATH NOTIFICATION

WHOSE CHILD IS THIS?

DESPITE A BLESSED REUNION WITH HIS WIFE AND TWO CHILDREN, A boy and a girl, Chaplain Tim Parker's return to stateside duty in Colorado was not a true respite. He no longer heard distant bursts of gunfire or worried that mortars might fall from the sky and pulverize him. Without the noise of war, though, the sound of familiar human suffering only seemed louder.

Soon after arriving at Fort Carson, he was assigned a death notification visit. With a casualty assistance officer named Smither, the chaplain drove to a quiet residential area, parked on the street, then in full dress uniform made the long walk from curbside to the doorstep.

The soldier's wife, Wendy, opened the door holding an infant. She immediately knew why they were there.

"No, no-o-o. . ."

A slender teenaged girl with long dark hair appeared behind Wendy, her face frozen in shock as Smither recited the official introduction and grievous news. He offered condolences and gratitude for the soldier's service. Wendy stood silent for a long and uncomfortable minute, then turned to the girl.

"Clara, take the baby. Officers, please come in."

The chaplain was there to give emotional and moral support

to the family and sometimes to the officer, who may be nervous because he hasn't had much experience in this area. Once the visitors were seated, Wendy glanced at Clara, who stood rocking the child.

"How did he…pass?"

"Ma'am, at this time we don't have a definitive … narrative," the officer said. She lowered her face into her hands.

"But he has a son. A son he's never met." Again, condolences were offered.

Wendy looked up at the chaplain. "Does it matter?"

"Uh … pardon?"

"If I know exactly how my husband died, would that be better spiritually, or would it only bring more pain?"

"Well, the details can be distressing. Yet …" the officer stalled, gathering his thoughts. "Yet we're human and can't help but want to know."

She turned to Clara. "Do you want to know, Honey?"

The daughter seemed surprised to be put on the spot. "Well, I already know he won't be coming home."

"Actually, he will be," the chaplain reminded her.

"Oh. Right."

Her father's body was scheduled to arrive in a couple days at nearby Peterson Air Force Base. There would be a ceremony when the family received their fallen loved one.

Wendy, eyes still on her daughter, said, "But you won't be able to … talk to him again. You won't be able to . . ."

"I talk to him every day, Mom. Why should that have to change?"

Wendy nodded, dazed, already in mourning. "Would you attend the ceremony, Chaplain?"

It was an unusual request. Typically, after the notification, another chaplain would be assigned the airport reception and funeral.

"Of course. If that's what you would like."

"Yes. Please."

The Army notification team never knew how next of kin would respond. Extremely emotional or stoic. Break down or shut down. Or both.

Wendy froze, as though perched on a precipice. The chaplain leaned forward, to catch her or at least break the fall should she collapse. Smither was equally alert.

Then she sat back and stared beyond her visitors, eyes watering, chest heaving. The chaplain wondered: *Did scenes from their life together rush by? Did she recall her husband's smile at their wedding or hear his jokes? Could she dare to admit, now at this moment, that what she thought was her future would be buried with her husband*?

Wendy reached toward Clara, who understood and gently handed her mother the baby. "You have big shoes to fill, little man," Wendy whispered. "Big shoes."

Clara's lips trembled, but she wouldn't let herself cry. Abruptly, she disappeared into another room.

Later in the week, Capt. Parker traveled with the family to the air base to receive the soldier's remains. The solemn event, like so many military rituals, felt ancient, a continuum of honor and dignity.

On the way to funeral home, people filled the streets, stopping to show respect as the hearse went by. The chaplain was moved, as though the loss was entirely his own. The next day he conducted the funeral and included several Scriptures from John 14.

"Let not your heart be troubled; you believe in God, believe also in Me. In My Father's house are many mansions; if it were not so, I would have told you. . .I will come again and receive you to Myself; that where I am, there you may be also… A little while longer and the world will see Me no more, but you will see Me. Because I live, you will live also… Peace I leave with you, My peace I give to you; not as the world gives do I give to you. Let not your heart be troubled, neither let it be afraid"(John 14:1-2a-3;19, 27, NKJV)[1]

The service seemed to go exceptionally well; it was one of

those times when the chaplain felt like he was standing in for God to help a hurting family. It was a good feeling, but a scary one too. Giving comfort and pointing them to God was a good thing, but thinking that he— by his great skill and wisdom—had fixed things wasn't right. He wasn't God, and only He could genuinely restore this wounded family.

After the service, he bid Wendy and her family farewell and assumed he'd never see them again. He was wrong. Later that year, Fort Carson organized a ceremony for families that had lost a loved one in recent months. Afterword, the chaplain noticed familiar faces and made eye contact with Wendy as she mingled with her family and friends. He was sure she recognized him. Yet the widow seemed to avoid him.

As the hall emptied, the chaplain turned toward the altar to mask his struggle with conflicting emotions. He was sensitive to how Wendy might feel, but he did not like being shunned. The experience left him feeling hollow and alone, wondering if he'd done something to offend the family. Then he heard the voice.

"Chaplain."

He turned. "Hello, Clara. I noticed you arrive. How are you and your brother?"

She pursed her lips and looked down to avoid answering. "I wanted to say … I apologize for my mom."

"No, no."

"Yes. You've been so good to us. But she … she couldn't … visit with you."

"Of course," he said, and felt hypocritical for pretending to be unhurt.

"I mean, *I get it*, I guess. It's time for her to move on and every reminder …"

"Yes, yes."

"And yet you're like family."

He felt tears forming. *Please Lord, not now.*

Mute, suppressing the sensation of joy tarnished with a dash of shame, he nodded. "Chaplain … there's another reason she couldn't face you."

"Oh?"

Clara turned pale as she confessed, "The baby isn't my brother. He's mine. I knew I was pregnant last time Dad was home, but … I … I …"

"You couldn't tell him."

"Yes! And now I wish I could!"

"Of course."

"But he's gone!"

The 17-year-old, who looked like a younger version of Wendy, threw her arms around the chaplain and sobbed, her face pressed against the cross on his uniform.

"I miss Daddy. Every day. I talk to him. But I wish I didn't have to let go. I wish I could be strong—like you."

––––––

COL. BRAND ANSWERED on the second ring. It was getting late in his part of the country, but he rarely ignored a call. And by now, he recognized this phone number.

"Thank you for taking my call, Sir."

"Of course. Enjoying the Rockies?"

A nervous laugh, then silence, then a deep sigh before Tim Parker could speak. "The attainments … they … sometimes I feel like I'm in a race, and then I cross the finish line and feel so good. But then it's like I've slipped backward and never finished the race and … my feelings are so …"

"Have you ever been on a boat at sea?"

"Yes."

"Was it always smooth sailing?"

"No."

"Of course not. The vessel rocks and if you have the muscle strength, you do your best to stay upright and keep your balance. But you can't just stand there. Something much bigger is in control. You're just along for the ride."

"Or for a drenching."

"Yes, that's possible. But in your case, it seems you've weathered the storm."

"I'm not so sure. I work hard to be good at what I do. Some days I just feel beat up."

"But not by others."

"No."

"Yourself."

"Mmm."

Brand liked to talk, not lecture. As a young man, he hated to be barked at by his elders, who seemingly had every solution for life's troubles at the tips of their tongues. My, how they could go on. So he asked questions and let his protégé do the talking. He learned about the funeral, the shunning, and about a host of other encounters that might drain most any caregiver, given their frequency and stubborn refusal to be resolved.

"It's the spouses, Chaplain Brand. They are left behind to contend with the wreckage. In some ways, they have it harder than soldiers who are at war. Because they must do everything the couple used to do together."

The chaplain went on, naming a long list of responsibilities left to wives and significant others: raising and disciplining the children, finances, home and car repairs, household chores, handling every little crisis, transporting kids to events, holding down a paying job, and …

"The men and women overseas face danger, but they have all their basic needs taken care of. They also have a clearly defined mission and all the resources necessary to complete it," he went on. "Best of all, they have each other. A sense of camaraderie. But recently I've spoken to so many wives who don't get much support at all. It makes me feel . . ."

"Like you're on a boat in the middle of a wind-blown sea."

"Yes."

"OK. When you were on a boat at sea, and it got rough, you didn't swim to shore and then criticize yourself because you couldn't stand upright."

"Mmm. Now I get it."

"Do you? Because when we're rocked emotionally, we mistakenly believe we're weak and not good at what we do. When, in fact, there must be some give and take. An accommodation. Rigidity is not a solution, in my opinion, but discipline is. And awareness. Experiencing all these feelings is difficult, but feeling nothing would render you useless to your community."

Parker now felt foolish for calling. Why couldn't he work out these things for himself?

He was always the schooner with broken masts being towed to harbor by a tugboat.

"So ... am I missing the point? Is what you're describing another attainment, Col. Brand?"

"No, not quite. But before I explain, Army chaplains are deployed here and there and asked to deal with whatever comes their way. Sometimes I think we'd be better to see ourselves as pastors of a large flock. We must learn to manage the parish, so to speak, and this is true regardless of whether you're Christian, Muslim, Jewish, Buddhist, whatever. Instead, sometimes we focus on one problem at a time and ..."

"It's exhausting."

"Don'cha know!"

Brand promised to send some books he thought would provide further guidance. Before he could sign off, the younger chaplain interrupted.

"But my question about ..."

"Ah, yes. The attainments. They are markers, milestones. But without a context ..."

Silence. Capt. Parker stared at his phone, believing he'd lost his connection. Then Brand began to speak again, seemingly with a heavy heart.

"Oh, my."

Concerned, the young man asked, "Is there a problem?"

"Yes."

"I've kept you too long."

"No, no. The problem is I'm about to mix my metaphors." Again, a bit of shared laughter.

"Look, I'm not a big fan of sports analogies, but I must admit they're often convenient. So here goes. Think of a football field."

"I like football."

"All right, then. Think of the attainments as markings—the fifty-or thirty-yard line—or the end zones."

"OK."

"Now ask yourself, what good would they be without the grass?"

---

1. 1 **New King James Version (NKJV)**
   Scripture taken from the New King James Version®. Copyright © 1982 by Thomas Nelson. Used by permission. All rights reserved.

7

AGELESS WISDOM

PHYSICIANS OF THE HEART

TIM PARKER WAS INTRIGUED WHEN HE RECEIVED A PACKAGE FROM Col. Brand that included writings by Pope Gregory I.

Hmmm. What could a Roman Catholic pope who lived 1400 years ago possibly have to say that could help me —a Protestant chaplain— serve warriors of the 21st Century?

Then he noticed a note from Brand. It read, "Take a look at this one. Gregory made a significant contribution to pastoral care with his tome, *The Book of Pastoral Rule.* His ideas are still relevant today."

Capt. Parker started reading and was surprised at the illuminating wisdom of this man who lived during the Dark Ages. The chaplain always thought the higher one rose in church leadership, the more vulnerable he became to the "I am God" temptation. Surely being pope would make one feel that kind of power. But Gregory had a clear sense of his boundaries.

He recognized a clear division between secular authority and spiritual leadership. He understood the emperor was God's representative for secular authority and church leaders were responsible for religious affairs. He encouraged each to focus on his own sphere.

One exception was his view that religious leaders be advocates for weak and innocent people. Gregory allowed church leaders to intercede for those treated unjustly by the government.

In his book of pastoral guidelines, this man who became known as Gregory the Great challenged bishops and priests to be "physicians of the heart." One of his most significant concepts in conducting pastoral care is that no two cases are exactly alike. He argued that no clear-cut answer fits every circumstance. Capt. Parker could relate. He always wanted to have a set of reliable solutions for the common problems his soldiers faced, but that never seemed to work.

The chaplain also was intrigued by Gregory's observation that what someone considers a virtue may be a vice. For instance, a person who takes pride in frugality may be expressing the sin of miserliness. A pastor would need to help that person peel back layers of self-deception by expanding their consciousness—through listening, patient support, and occasional advice.

Gregory espoused a balance between caring for how persons feel and changing outward behaviors. God's care gives people the temporary satisfaction of feeling better about themselves. His higher purpose, however, is the long-term reforming of beliefs and habits. Gregory advised pastors to influence incremental and constructive changes in their parishioners, so their happiness was more abundant and grounded. He said Christ is the true Pastor, doing the deep work of transformation, while pastors here on Earth are a mere extension of God's caring.

The chaplain paused to reflect. He thought of Daniel Roth, the intel officer who blamed himself for a lost mission. When he counseled Roth, wasn't he carrying out Pope Gregory's idea of reforming beliefs and habits? And, if given the time, wouldn't he have tried to do the same with Sgt. Matt Kennedy? The chaplain's best hope of helping that brave soldier was in challenging Kennedy's thoughts about God.

He gave himself a modest pat on the back, then continued reading.

Gregory taught a lot about power and authority. He argued that a pastor's authority is paradoxically authenticated through humble service using Jesus as the model. He said pastors should "Consider in themselves not the authority of their rank, but the quality of their condition, and to rejoice not to be over [persons], but to do them good."

Gregory elaborated on his ideas of pastoral authority. On the one hand, pastors and parishioners are not equal in the same way parent and child or teacher and learner are not equal. On the other hand, caring for souls presumes a fundamental equality of the human condition.

Aware of this dilemma, he warned of the dangers of pride for those who provided guidance. "Pastors can begin to think more of themselves than they should, forgetting their basic equality with those to whom they provide guidance."

The chaplain now scolded himself for that pat on the back. *So prideful.* Then he read another quote that sent his head spinning.

Gregory concluded, "He orders this power well who knows both how to maintain it and to combat it."

What a paradox! The pope was telling pastors to, at the same time, maintain and resist pastoral authority.

Gregory also highlighted the importance of the pastor's heart. He was aware that pastors needed to deal with their own issues. One danger he identified was that pastors become so involved in their parishioners' struggles they lose objectivity and self-awareness. The pope wrote, "Having intense concern for others may dissipate the concentration of the mind." It is as though one were "so preoccupied during a journey as to forget what one's destination was."

Aha! thought the chaplain. He too had struggled with objectivity.

Gregory had two recommendations for pastors to assist them in protecting their hearts from self-deception and lack of self-awareness. First, he encouraged pastors to spend time contemplating truths of the Bible, renewing their minds and hearts so that they would gain a better understanding of truth and to discern the thoughts of God. Second, he recommended continuous self-examination under the care of another experienced pastoral guide.

Parker no longer felt so self-conscious for having reached out so many times to Col. Brand. How lucky he was to have a mentor! And it wasn't a relationship he knew on his own to pursue. He believed Providence had brought him and his teacher together.

He was getting sleepy now, but Gregory's advice to pastors continued to rock his consciousness. The next blast was a warning to pastors against advocating merely for what a parishioner wants. Instead, he recommends pastors guide parishioners to what they ought to want, to draw them to the truth.

Gregory also warned against pastoral activism that "delights in being hustled by worldly tumults" and is "ignorant of the things that are within." He reminded pastors to focus on inner discipline and spiritual formation. He argued that pastors cannot provide proper counsel towards happiness if they do not themselves know the way.

The chaplain spoke aloud, "Know the way." And to himself, he added, *Know the way out of powerlessness.*

He put down the materials Brand had sent and marvelled that guidelines created centuries ago could prove so meaningful in his role as Army chaplain. He recognized these insights could be helpful to caregivers of all kinds. Doctors, nurses, police officers, parents, clergy, therapists, and counselors might improve their effectiveness and peace of mind if only they were willing to clarify their "pastoral" identities.

Pope Gregory's ideas had survived the test of time. Yet how soon would the chaplain be rocked again by the perplexing nature of his mission?

He put that worry to rest. It was time for bed.

8

DRONE TALLY

I am not powerless when I respect my beliefs.

CHAPLAIN TALLY GRIMES USUALLY DID NOT LOOK HER AGE WHICH was 40. She had a friendly face with blue eyes that sparkled when she spoke. Her laugh often caused her head to kickback as though she had just pulled the trigger on an M16.

Today as they sat together on a park bench, Parker noticed an aged weariness as he studied her face for signs of conflict or regret.

"Are you sure?" he said.

"Yes."

"What does your husband say?"

"He'd like to have me home more often," Grimes smirked.

"Selfish."

They both laughed, but the mirth quickly faded. Each stared toward the playground which was far enough away they could barely hear the voices of joy and silly fun.

Capt. Parker had always been impressed with Chaplain Grimes' bearing. She handled herself well in all situations, or so it seemed, and she had moved up the ranks rather swiftly. She got it—the Army, its traditions; its strengths and weaknesses; its glacier-like speed of change.

But now she was in trouble. She'd been reprimanded for an outburst that was atypical for this veteran, the daughter of an Episcopal priest.

"You're not being forced to leave, are you?"

She paused before answering. "Force comes in lots of shapes and ways and means. Sometimes you feel the wind at your back. Other times it's slapping you in the face. If the memorandum of reprimand stays in my file ... heck ... goodbye promotions. A mention of my big mouth will probably show up in every evaluation I have from here to eternity."

"So?" Parker was only suggesting that hard times did not preclude serving. In a year, who knew, maybe ruffled feathers would be soothed.

"Yeah, I get it. Life happens—even in the Army." A quick grin softened the impatience in her voice. "But what am I doing? What is my soul telling me I must do to be at peace with myself?"

The chaplain waited for an answer that did not come. He probed further, as a friend who feared she might be rash in her decision.

"A resignation is final, Tally. Isn't it a little soon to...?"

"No. It is not too soon to know, in a flash, who I am and what I stand for. Come on Tim, we know collateral damage happens all the time in war. But is an apology from our leadership ever enough? 'Oops. Sorry.' What if your kids had been in that village when the drone struck?"

Her question scored a direct hit. She knew she was correct in saying the American people were often too removed from the realities of war. They thanked their warriors for their courage and didn't lose sleep over the innocent lives obliterated by one miscalculation of a distant drone operator sitting in an air-conditioned technology center.

A boy in the playground leaped off his swing seat and

plunged head-first into the sand. As he bawled, a swarm of mothers came to his aid.

"Powerlessness," he whispered.

"What?"

"Does it make you feel powerless when the weapons of war go wacky?"

Her brow wrinkled. "I'm not sure what you're asking, Tim."

Ever the diplomat, he complimented her first. He said how impressed he'd been when they first met years before at school and how thankful he was for their friendship and professional camaraderie, even while being deployed to distant lands.

"But Tally, I've got to ask … you always seem so *together*. Nothing ever seems to phase you."

"Until now?"

"That's what I'm asking. When that reporter asked you those questions, didn't you know it could hurt if you misspoke?"

"But I didn't misspeak. I knew exactly what I was doing. I even put some heat into the delivery. I never thought it would go viral, but … hey."

Major Tally Grimes had not exposed herself with a firebrand Tweet or blog post. It happened when a reporter for the local television station followed some chaplain corps initiates through their infantry training. On camera, the reporter asked how pastors reconciled combat exercises with their faith. Thou Shalt Not Kill and other biblical pronouncements were thrown freestyle into the conversations.

Only Chaplain Grimes commented. She was a supervisor and not shy in answering questions about policy and procedures. The drone strike in Afghanistan had made headlines only days before.

"We're entitled to protest," she told the reporter. "We can draw a line in the sand. We can call out an atrocity for what it is — the willful mass murder of innocents. Unlawful. Immoral. We can be witnesses to the mindless things the United States of America too often condones in the name of self-defense."

There was not much reaction after the initial broadcast. Then a cable TV station featured it in a political show about national security issues. Suddenly, her face and vociferous condemnation were everywhere. TV networks and radio stations requested more interviews. She might have agreed, had the public relations officer, with the backing of the base commander, not shut her down.

"If I'd done a couple more interviews I would have forced the Army's hand. They may have discharged me."

"Or not. Wouldn't that only bring more bad PR?"

"Yeah, maybe."

"The point is they didn't kick you out. So why leave after all you've put into this?"

Tally stood and pointed to a pond beyond the playground. "Want to walk a little?"

"Sure."

"When I was growing up, my dad was assigned to an affluent congregation in a college town. The church architecture and surroundings were Norman Rockwell perfect. Dad was excited because it had all been made possible by the priest who had grown his flock with inspiring sermons and community outreach. He was kind of a mentor to my father. For several years all was well, though I know Dad felt a bit, um, exasperated by the main priest's style. He was an entertainer. A late-night-talk-show host in robes. He made faith and religion so easy, so digestible."

"Accessible."

"Yeah, but Dad's point was that even the most generous, loyal congregants needed to be challenged a bit more. He told me all this later, of course, after the fall."

"Whose fall?"

Chaplain Grimes skipped a couple stones across the surface of the pond and then continued walking along the edge of the water.

"The church enjoyed generous tithing and sponsored all

kinds of community groups, even a controversial theater troupe. It was a pretty liberal place. But not *that* liberal."

Tim realized he had begun to hold his breath as he sensed a turn in Tally's story. "What do you mean?"

"Sex."

"The congregants couldn't have sex?"

She laughed. "Yeah. Try winning fans with that. I mean, come on, these are Episcopalians we're talking about."

He wasn't quite sure what the joke was, but he was interested in hearing about the fall.

"See, one of the lady administrators, she'd been with the church forever, came to my father and said she needed someone to talk to. Someone who would be discreet."

The rest of the story unfolded quickly. The senior priest had been having sex with unhappy young housewives who had turned to him for counsel. They had succumbed to the priest's rationalization that he was leading them into a deeper type of spiritual guidance.

"Dad was conflicted. He knew he had to report this man— who had helped bring him to the church—but he also feared he too might be tainted for …"

"Blowing the whistle."

"Yeah. The new guy in town ruining a good thing. And, hey, he loved the place, his family was secure and so on. But more women began to seek him out, and he could see the damage the priest had done—to confused husbands, the children in the families, and the women themselves who were being manipulated by a so-called man of God."

"But what does this have to do with your situation?"

"Oh. Sorry. I'll get to that."

She said her father was singled out for reporting the sins, though it had not been him who anonymously called the local newspaper. When confronted, the senior priest lied. The parish was rocked and furiously divided.

"Dad was rocked too. He wondered if maybe he was part of

the problem. Why hadn't he seen the abuse sooner? And though he'd been forthright, he'd wrestled with his convictions and conscience and doubted his right to speak."

"And so?" Again, Parker sought some clarity.

Tally Grimes stopped and turned toward her friend. "I've never really had to take a stand on much. Not like my dad did, when you are risking something you love. Then all the casualties started getting to me. The deaths, the divorces, the broken lives. When do we finally say, enough already? Tell me, Tim, when do we draw a line and say this is not right? The drone thing, it's happening right now. We're taking people out, assassinations, like it's a video game. I'm not OK with it. I can't look the other way anymore."

"But leaving …?"

"On my own terms."

Tim Parker flashed on Pope Gregory's call for pastors to draw people to the truth. It would seem Tally's father had done as much, and now she was following his example.

On the other hand, the pope had also warned against pastoral activism that "delights in being hustled by worldly tumults." Was Tally Grimes teetering toward her own fall from grace by challenging her nation's modern military defense system?

The silence was broken by a gaggle of children rushing toward the pond. One little boy turned to the chaplains, noticed their uniforms and saluted. They returned his gesture.

"You mentioned powerlessness earlier," she said. "How come?"

"I've been talking about it a lot with other chaplains. We've all struggled with it. I wondered if it was something that has ever frustrated you."

She took her time to answer. "I know Dad felt it. When he told me about the scandal, I remember him saying, 'I felt powerless.' He wanted everybody to get what they deserved and be well, a kind of immaculate restoration of the community. But, finally, he realized all he could do was meet with church leadership and report what he knew."

"Haven't you already done that with your situation? You spoke your mind and took a hit. The memorandum of reprimand should be your badge of honor."

"It isn't. Agreeing to shut up because I'm afraid of my career stalling is not acceptable." Parker realized he was trying to keep his friend in the Chaplain Corps. That wasn't fair.

She needed to make her own decision. He nodded in acceptance and began walking toward the parking area. She moved with him.

"Where is your father now?" he asked.

"Well, some parishioners were not happy with Dad. But he stayed, eventually won over his critics, then he was promoted."

"He's top dog now?"

"He would describe it differently, but, yes, he's the presiding priest."

Capt. Parker stopped. "There you go. Hang in there. All will be well."

"No, my friend," she countered. "My father had no gripe with the institution or the Episcopalian liturgy. I know I won't change our military's policies or methods. The president of the United States isn't going to pardon me. But I feel complicit if I stay on and shut up. You asked me about powerlessness."

"Yes."

"I am *not* powerless when I respect my beliefs, my values. I can't force them on everybody else, but I can express them. In public. Without fear."

9

THE THIRD ATTAINMENT

GOD'S PROVIDENCE

TIM PARKER HATED TO BOTHER COL. BRAND WITH MORE QUESTIONS, but once again, he had hit a wall in understanding the attainments his mentor had outlined. Seminary had taught him to define Providence as "the foreseeing care and guidance of God in directing human affairs." But in the chaos and calamity of war, such care and guidance were hard to spot. *How many of our soldiers really believe Providence brought them to Iraq or Afghanistan? And was it Providence that took a good soldier like Tally Grimes out of the Army?*

With more questions spinning through his mind, he speed-dialed the number.

"Hi there, Tim. Good to hear from you. How are you doing with the books I sent?"

"I'm getting through them. Slowly, but carefully."

"So what's on your mind today?"

"It's the Third Attainment. I'm not seeing much evidence of Providence in the lives of the people I work with. I keep wanting to fix things for them. I know I can't, but it's hard to trust that everything will work out in the end."

"I understand. We hate to witness pain and injustice and not respond. Indifference, it would seem, is a bigger sin than intervening."

Brand reminded the chaplain that the second attainment, "I am *not* God," admonishes us for overreaching our humanity. "Meanwhile the third attainment asks us to embrace God as the answer to pain and injustice," Chaplain Brand said, "To recognize that God is all-powerful and has an ultimate plan for our lives."

"So was it God's plan for Major Grimes to leave the Army?"

"No, you misunderstand Providence. Often it's when God turns something we perceive as bad into something good. I respect Major Grimes' decision. It's the Army's loss. But she has a pastor's heart, and God will lead her into some other valuable form of service."

Parker pondered his friend's answer in an extended silence.

"You have to take a long view on things like this, Tim. Never forget what the Bible says in Romans 8:28, '… that God causes all things to work together for good to those who love God, to those who are called according to *His* purpose.[1] You can influence the outcome for your friend by praying for her. Don't ever stop praying for people in your care."

"Thanks. I know these things. But living them is not so easy."

"I want to suggest something else that may help. Talk to some other chaplains in your Corps. Ask how they view Providence in their work."

"OK, I will. And I will keep reading too."

"Good. Not all the books I sent have a Christian worldview, but they all have tools that can help you minister to hurting people."

In the weeks that followed that phone call, Capt. Parker spoke to over a dozen chaplains.

Their responses surprised him. The Providence attainment seems to give chaplains a sense of hope and the ability to persevere. His colleagues used these statements to describe its impact on their ministry:

1. "I'm reminded of truths in the Bible, God is in control."
2. "It is hard to wait, but God's timing is perfect—a matter of faith."
3. "I don't let it overwhelm me. God's still there, He wins. Period."
4. "He's unlimited... knows all...sees and is the whole picture."
5. "God knows the purpose...He makes the end beautiful."
6. "Who knows how God is allowing life events to work?"
7. "Things happen for good, out of chaos and evil...His end, His goal is accomplished...through Christ's power."

Parker came to realize his own belief in God's Providence had been challenged by the tragic results of violence, accidents, and hurtful stupidity. *Only God knows why these things keep happening. They happen regardless of whether I understand. I can grieve over them or accept them, but acceptance should not be equated with indifference.*

How do frontline caregivers (police, paramedics, firefighters, military medics, and ER personnel) handle these challenges? He wondered. *They are in the business of saving lives, but do they also struggle with grief and acceptance when a life is lost or left so broken that they wonder whether they should have saved it?*

He felt a little envious of first responders. They get to move on to other cases after saving a life, while other medical providers—social workers, counselors, and clergy—are left to heal their broken hearts and broken dreams. *Yes, sometimes those are harder to fix than broken bodies.* The chaplain concluded that all caregivers share a bond as healers and purveyors of hope. All can utilize the power of the Divine to resolve their feelings of powerlessness. To trust in Providence means giving the broken person confidence that God can bring good out of whatever painful thing has happened to them.

One book sent by Col. Brand struck him as odd because of its title. Tim Parker wondered how a book called *Power Is the Great Motivator* by Harvard professor David C. McClelland, could help people struggling with powerlessness and the need to depend on God. To his surprise, he found some relationship between McClelland's theories and the attainments.

Two decades after Abraham Maslow developed his revolutionary pyramid showing the hierarchy of human needs, Dr. McClelland presented his own Achievement Motivation Theory. The distinguished behavioral scientist identified three motivators he believed we all have: a need for achievement, a need for affiliation, and a need for power. He found people would have different characteristics depending on their dominant motivator. Later in his career, McClelland focused more of his study on the inner experiences of power. After all the chaplain's own struggles with powerlessness, this immediately hooked his attention.

In his power motivation theory, McClelland defined stages of growth he calls power orientation. In the first stage of his model, the person is empowered and strengthened from something outside the self, which is a form of dependency. Individuals draw their feeling of power/strength from being around influential people. It can also come from being associated with God or some religious power.

The second stage is described as "I strengthen myself." In this phase, people look to themselves as a source of their power. They strive to feel autonomous and in control of themselves. The chaplain laughed when he read that McClelland identified psychologists as a typical example of this stage. He said they feel powerful by learning what makes people tick. This gives them a better understanding of themselves, and, as a result, more control.

The third stage of McClelland's power orientation model is characterized as "I have an impact on others." This stage can have both a negative and positive force. One person uses their influence to assert control over others while another is fulfilled by helping others. Solving a problem for someone else makes all people in this stage feel powerful.

The fourth and final stage is titled "It moves me to do my duty." People in this stage are empowered by obligating themselves to causes and circumstances outside of themselves. They see themselves as an instrument of a higher power in which they serve and influence others.

They have learned the dictum: "Yield to a higher authority, serve it, and you will feel happy and strong."

Stage four is considered the mature stage. McClelland suggests that individuals who have attained this level answer the power-powerlessness dilemma by committing to some authority or purpose higher than themselves. Maturity is demonstrated when people who have worked all the way through the stages are able to use each one appropriately based on the situation. Immaturity is displayed by using one platform in all circumstances or using the stages improperly.

McClelland's work helped Chaplain Parker realize his friend Tally Grimes was not doubting God, she was questioning a powerful nation's methods of defense. She was, in her own way, attempting to embrace the greater good by yielding to a higher authority, the teachings of Christ. Therefore, she had no fear of reprisals.

After reading McClelland's book, the chaplain fired off an email to thank his friend—not only for the book, but for helping him work through his feelings related to Tally Grimes. A thread of emails followed, allowing Col. Brand to comment on McClelland's theory and to give more insight into his views about powerlessness and Providence. The latest email deeply touched Chaplain Parker:

My friend, it does not matter how much chaplains and

other caregivers refine their skills. There will always be instances when they are powerless.

But learn everything you can about this condition. Dr. McClelland offers a theory that *assists* caregivers when in the throes of this crippling kind of experience. A broader perspective of powerlessness gives us the courage to acknowledge its presence. "I am powerless." Now we are no longer fighting it, but we are "one" with it. There is no conflict.

Once that has happened, we take command of ourselves only, and we open our hearts to God's Providence.

Respectfully,
Robert Brand

---

1. 2 **New American Standard Bible (NASB)**
   Copyright © 1960, 1962, 1963, 1968, 1971, 1972, 1973, 1975, 1977, 1995 by The Lockman Foundation

ACTIVE SHOOTER

"I don't want to be married to this."

MELBA WAS CALM AND FRIENDLY AT FIRST, WILLING TO SUBMIT TO the chaplain's questions, some of which challenged her recent decision to file for divorce. Chaplain Parker had met her months before at the request of Sgt. Deshawn Jefferson, her husband. The chaplain liked her then, and he liked her still, even though she now went silent, folding her strong brown arms and clenching her jaw, an attempt to say without words that she could not be swayed.

"See?" Deshawn said. "She won't talk. She's on her own planet now. She's spinning out of orbit."

The chaplain took no side, though he was inclined to agree. Before he could respond, she did.

"I don't have to talk just because you have questions. There were times when I didn't hear from you for weeks."

"I was overseas."

"You had your phone. The Army has computers."

"We were in-country. It wasn't smart to be calling home asking, *whaddup?*"

"I'll tell you whaddup. I'm done talking about this. There's nothing more to say. How many times do we have to come back here?"

"Till we make things better," he said.

"I don't want *better*. I want different."

Deshawn, beaten, looked at the chaplain, palms up.

"Melba ... of course you don't have to come back. But I would regret saying goodbye today, to both of you, without first being sure that you know ..."

"What I'm doing?" Now her voice had a sharp edge. "See, that's what I find so annoying.

You think I don't know what I'm doing. Deshawn, too. So let me give you a list of *what I'm doing*."

Melba's delivery was impressive for its clarity and speed. What she'd been doing was—

1. Raising three children without a father.
2. Writing a blog called *Army Family Meals on $5 a Day*.
3. Praying that her husband would not come home in a casket.
4. Searching for a second part-time job.
5. Volunteering at church.
6. Ignoring her own health.
7. Doing laundry, house cleaning, dishwashing.
8. Supporting Deshawn's little sister through first-boyfriend ecstasy and despair.
9. Watching her passion for life fade like the color in an old favorite dress.

"And that's only the short version of a big long list. I won't bore you with the parts about crying myself to sleep thinking I should end it all."

"Isn't that what you're doing now?" Deshawn interjected.

"No. I've got kids to raise. Killing myself is another luxury I can't afford, *D.*"

"That's not what I . . ."

"I know what you meant. But, no, I'm not *ending it all* by leaving this marriage. I'm ending my role as your patient wife. I'm saying *no* to you putting the welfare of your troops above that of your family."

"I'm defending freedom."

"Whose freedom? Not mine. I'm buried. We have no money. Our boy is struggling in school. The car shouldn't be on the road without new brakes and a tune-up. Thanks, buddy, now take out the garbage and drive the kids to school!"

Deshawn launched to his feet and kicked his chair away.

"Oh, great," Melba hissed. "Now have another meltdown because your wife *just doesn't understand.*"

He turned on her with a rage that pulled the chaplain to his feet.

"Deshawn!"

But the husband and soldier kept on shouting. When Capt. Parker finally got him seated again, Deshawn looked defeated.

"I'll try! OK? That's all I'm saying. Stay, and I'll try—again and again. Otherwise, I don't know how you're any better off with a divorce. What will you do? Run to your parents? Or get a new boyfriend?"

"Oh, God, just what I need. Another man to drain my batteries!"

The poised, persistent Melba was on her feet now, too, but the silence had returned. She turned as though to leave, then stopped and exhaled dramatically. Her face was pained, but not one tear fell.

Deshawn, the veteran warrior, now put his head against the wall and pounded it with his fist. An admittedly lousy husband, he was now torn in two by demands he could not fulfill.

The three stood in restless quiet until the chaplain finally spoke.

"OK ... all right ... I know this is difficult, but ... I feel lucky to be here." Man and wife looked at the caregiver as though his mind had curdled.

"No, I mean it. I'm lucky to hear things that ... to hear the things good people need to say. And I make a mistake—yeah, I make mistakes too—of trying to hold everything together. Find the glue. Don't let it break. Never let it break."

Initially, the chaplain felt as though he was wandering into a swamp. Now, after letting his own thoughts flow, he felt something underfoot that was a bit soggy but firm: his own truth.

"You see, it's hard to say to people, 'Hey, maybe you're right. Maybe the best thing to do is to admit this isn't working anymore.' But if I said that I'd worry that I'd let you down and had not done my job. Except, my job is not to keep you together."

He could tell he'd caught their attention, so he continued.

"No, you see, I just want to know that you've explored all as best you can. God knows, divorce is tough too. But if that's your choice, at least ... well ... maybe there's a little bit of deliverance? By just saying, uh huh, the leg just fell off the table, and that's why it crashed to the floor, isn't that better than ..." He struggled to finish, having lost his footing. "Know what I'm saying?"

Melba was smiling now, and finally, shedding some tears.

Deshawn shook his head. "Man, that ... *that* was ... the most ridiculous thing I've ever heard you say!"

Melba giggled, and then the chaplain felt a tickle and burst out laughing. The trio became a chorus of nonsensical glee, stepping closer for an improbable group hug.

Now the real talking began, and it was free of tension. If splitting was the final answer, they had to make plans for how and when. They would need to sit down with their children and reach out to extended family and friends. Both parents would need to think beyond the Army and consider career options that might provide for two households.

"Do I really want to be a career man in the Army?" Deshawn asked of himself.

Melba was sympathetic. "Look into some other training options, D. You're smart. You work well with other people."

"But…"

"I know it won't be easy. Emotionally. But…"

"Yeah."

"Am I right?"

Deshawn nodded, but it hurt. He was invested. Dug in. His eyes watered as he gritted his teeth. "Sometimes it's so hard to imagine tomorrow. Something different. I support my guys, but they hold me up too. If I walk away, I mean I know this sounds crazy, but will I just collapse?"

The chaplain answered softly. "Yes. You'll be like a ship without an anchor for a while."

Husband and wife gave him another look. Melba's was hardest to endure: She was hoping for support, encouragement.

"Deshawn, when the leg falls off the table…"

"Oh, don't start with that table b.s.!" he said, and pulled away.

The chaplain rushed to bring him back into the circle. "You're right, you're right. But listen. My only point is…"

"I'm not a freakin' piece of furniture. I'm a man. This hurts. A table doesn't feel a damn thing!"

I'm an idiot, the chaplain thought. *Christ, help me.* Then he took a deep breath and let Deshawn's seething fade to silence before speaking again.

"When things change, you feel awkward, out of balance. That's all I meant. I'm sorry if I offended you."

Melba waited, detached until Deshawn turned. He looked at his wife and opened his mouth to speak when an alarm blared. In the hallway, they heard shouting and heavy footsteps. They startled when someone pounded on the office door, then forced himself in. An armed soldier.

"Active shooter at the chow hall! Lock yourself in and don't come out until you hear an announcement!"

Then he was gone, moving down the corridor, repeating his orders. Melba panicked. "We have to get out of here."

"No," the chaplain said, his own mind wracked with violent memories of Iraq. "Get down, Melba."

"I'm not staying here!"

"Get down!"

Deshawn grabbed his wife and forced her behind the desk, and then rushed to the window. He surveyed the grounds as best he could and then pulled down the blinds and turned off the fluorescent overhead lights.

"You too, Chaplain. Hit the floor."

More shots were fired, and Chaplain Parker imagined the scene outside, bodies sprawled in pools of blood. The war had come home.

Deshawn sheltered his weeping wife with his body.

"All right, baby. We're cool. We're safe here. I'm a great big blanket wrapping you up. Like when we brought our babies home from the…"

Another burst of gunfire rocked the building. The chaplain pulled himself to his knees and began to pray, straining to be heard over the commotion. Faint shouting could be heard and then a prolonged barrage of automatic weapons fire.

"What the hell's going on?" Deshawn said.

The chaplain turned to see the soldier pull away from his wife, and crawl to the second- story window.

"I've got to get out there."

"No, Deshawn."

The chaplain rose to block the path to the door, but he was no match for the linebacker-like power of the combat veteran.

Melba pleaded, "Don't go, Deshawn. Please don't go."

"I've got guys out there."

The chaplain threw his arms around the soldier. "No. Come on, man. Not now. Not…"

"I can't let them get blown away!"

Deshawn tossed aside the chaplain, yanked open the door and raced toward danger.

Melba ran into the hallway, "Deshawn!"

"Melba, come back in."

The chaplain tried to pull her back to safety, but the mother of three pounded his chest, screaming.

"I don't want this life anymore!"

"The Bible says…"

"Don't tell me about the Bible! I don't want to be married to this!"

CHAPLAIN STATION

RESCUE THE LIVING

THE HELP CAME FROM ALL DIRECTIONS. THE ARMY BASE AS WELL AS the municipal police and fire departments with emergency medical staff. The shooter, a decorated Army infantryman who had suffered PTSD after three deployments in Afghanistan, had taken five lives, threatened a dozen hostages and forced the base into lockdown during a protracted negotiation with an FBI team. When the shooter raised the stakes by firing his weapon wildly and cutting off communication, the decision was made to storm the building.

That battle had been terrifying even for those who could only listen, unaware of the shoot-to-kill order that had been given.

Media would cover the event relentlessly in the days to come. The shooter's life would be examined in minute detail. Then the families of the victims would be interviewed for specifics about their loved ones. It would all seem so raw and stunning for a week or two. Locals would utter, "Let the healing begin." And then the ordeal would fade as the next "unimaginable" incident took precedent.

As he considered the heartbreaking patterns of recent shootings at schools, businesses, and public buildings, the chaplain wondered if the people who committed these crimes were like falling stars. They had died within or somehow been thrown out of orbit, only to make one big flash before spinning into darkness.

It was nearly dark when the "all clear' came, and Melba was processed and allowed to exit the grounds. She and the chaplain had waited in tense silence for three hours, and her husband never returned.

As he watched Melba drive off, Capt. Parker knew she'd be picking up the broken pieces of her family's life, a life without Deshawn. In some ways, it would be as painful as the loss felt by the families and friends of today's shooting victims.

Parker soon joined other chaplains and caregivers from the city—counselors, priests, ministers and community leaders—to create a station where survivors could speak about their experiences if they wished. He knew he would also be called upon to conduct funerals, visit the wounded, and counsel with families of the victims.

Yet it might be days or weeks before some of them could even express themselves.

Sometimes we want to run from our distress, the chaplain thought as if we could shake it off. But that wasn't possible for everyone. His first visit with Col. Brand had taught him that we store feelings, suppress them, only to be overwhelmed by painful memories at inopportune moments.

As men and women gathered to be debriefed, the chaplain heard pieces of conversation, shards of terror and incomprehension.

"He started shooting, like he was at a carnival."

"Was the shooter stationed here?"

"Somebody call my husband for me, I've lost my phone. I've lost, oh my God, I've nearly lost my mind. I can't function anymore."

Some counseling sessions were long and detailed, but not necessarily articulate. The trauma sometimes caused people to gush with recitations of every step leading up to the incident, past histories, appointments missed, and so forth. Other interactions were short, mere affirmations of being saved. The glory of still being alive.

Many exchanges were nothing more than an embrace, and a whispered *thank you* before boarding a bus. Good people who, for whatever reason, were not in the shooter's arc of death.

Yet through it all, the chaplain imagined the people he would likely never get close to: the shooter's circle of relations who now might come face to face with their own sense of powerlessness. Had they not seen the signs? Or had they tried to help but to no avail?

Hours passed as he engaged with other caregivers and marveled at the civilians who had rushed to their aid. So often some military personnel question whether anyone in America knows what troops face in distant lands to defend freedom. Yet here were some of the most thoughtful members of the community coming to their rescue.

Then the chaplain heard a familiar voice. "Why does this keep happening?"

The chaplain turned to see Deshawn and felt a tangle of emotions. He had no right to scold anyone and yet could feel something like that impulse gathering in him. Admiration and relief were also in the mix.

"I don't know, Deshawn. Were you in danger?"

"Didn't even get close. Pure chaos. Everybody's frazzled. But I don't think any of my people were involved." The admission seemed to make him shiver, or maybe it was the cold night descending on his broad shoulders. "Chaplain, am I ruining my life caring too much?"

"Don't you care about Melba?"

"Of course, I do. But nobody is pointing a gun at her head."

"Except you."

Deshawn was insulted but kept his cool. "*What?*"

"You won't change. You're saying to Melba that she must accept whatever you choose, even if it obviously harms your family. Don't you—or can't you—see that she's defending your home and children with the same fervor you defend your unit? Melba is a warrior too. But who sees her? She's not in uniform. She won't earn health benefits or be able to go school on the G. I. Bill for her commitment. But she deserves it, in my opinion."

The two stressed-out soldiers, men engaged in a heated exchange about commitment. Considering the day they had both survived it was not surprising that emotions were so raw. In the end, Deshawn Jefferson could only throw up his hands.

"What am I supposed to do, Chaplain?"

"I think you've already done it. You've made your choice. And, to me, it looks like Melba has too. I'm sorry, Deshawn. I ... I'm sorry I wasn't able to bring you both together again."

"Maybe nobody could."

Now the chaplain flinched: That phrase again, *nothing could be done*. He hated the sound of it, the implication that his work was always in vain.

"You're married, aren't you?" Deshawn's question surprised him.

"Yes."

"You ever mess up?"

He felt exposed; like a spotlight had suddenly found him trying to escape. The chaplain's mind now spun like a carousel, replaying his mistakes and the times his devoted wife had had to set him straight. He was no stranger to coming up short. And what, at first, had felt like a smack to the face now only made him ticklish. He laughed.

"Messed up? Oh, man, Deshawn. Let me count the ways."

———

THE DIVORCE WAS FINAL. That was the last Capt. Parker heard from Deshawn and Melba Jefferson. Deshawn soon deployed back to Iraq. Melba moved off base and got a better-paying job at a local hospital. Tim felt sadness every time he thought of them.

God, I know You hate it when families break up and individual lives shatter. Why does it keep happening?

He thought of them often over the next two years and prayed for them each time he did.

Then one day he got an unexpected call.

"You got time to talk with an old divorced husband?" the voice inquired.

"Is that you, Deshawn?"

"Yeah, Chaplain, I'm back in town. I'd like to meet with you again."

"Can you come by my office at ten tomorrow?"

"I can meet then, but not your place. Too many bad memories for me. Let's do the Starbucks outside the base entrance."

The chaplain was stunned to see Deshawn stride up the next day wearing shorts, with a prosthetic leg fully exposed. Deshawn reached out his hand with a friendly smile.

Tim shook his hand and said, "What happened?"

"Damned IED got me. Right after deploying to Afghanistan. I'm out of the Army now."

"I'm so sorry, I know how much it meant to you, being with your men."

"Yeah, the divorce was bad enough. When this happened, and I knew my Army days were over, I wanted to end it all."

"But you didn't. Why?"

"It may sound funny, but it's because God gave me my life back, different than it was before."

"What do you mean?"

"I was so bitter and angry after my leg got blown off. I hated life. I didn't want to talk to anybody. Then my kids started writing to me. I think Melba encouraged them to do it. Anyway, those letters were life to me. My son said he was proud of me, that he loved me, and that God loved me too. Can you believe that? After all the pain I caused those kids. It ripped my heart."

"So how did you respond?"

"I'm not much of a writer. So one day I worked up the

courage to call them. Melba answered, and I thanked her for allowing them to write to me. She said they never stopped loving me—that it was their idea to write and encourage me. I lost it on the phone after that. I asked her to forgive me, and when she did, I blubbered like a baby. I've talked to them every day since then. When my rehab was done, I decided to move back here. Melba let me move back in with them. I'm sharing a room with my son Dontrell."

"That's amazing. It sounds to me like God's Providence. He takes that which was our greatest pain and somehow uses it for our good."

"I don't know that word, but I know I've got my family back. Better than before. Different than before. I want to thank you for praying for Melba and me and the kids. I know you were frustrated that you couldn't fix our marriage back when we first came to you. I was so damned hardheaded then, I doubt you could have cracked my skull with a two-by-four, let alone my heart. It took God and the kids to do that."

"Thank you for sharing this Deshawn. I'm so happy for you. And I intend to keep praying for you and Melba and the kids. I think God has more providential things in store for you."

1 2

BRAND'S CONFESSION

AMBUSH

CHAPLAIN PARKER COULDN'T WAIT TO TELL HIS FRIEND AND MENTOR about the breakthrough in Deshawn and Melba Jefferson's marriage. "They're still divorced but what a difference from the last time I met together with them! Melba was cold as a mama polar bear; Deshawn was all into himself and the Army.

When I described what that meeting was like for me, they nodded their heads and smiled. Then we all started laughing. We laughed so hard that my sides hurt.

"I was embarrassed afterward. I mean this couple has endured so much loss and strain ... laughing felt unprofessional."

"Mm hm. How many hours had you been on your feet by then?"

"Oh, God ..."

"That long, huh?"

The chaplain smiled, and he guessed his mentor on the other end of the telephone call was doing the same thing.

"It's odd, isn't it? At times, laughter might be the most effective coping mechanism we have when we feel powerless. Not laughing in someone's face, or jeering or, you know, making fun of others. But surrendering."

"To the absurdity?"

"That could be."

"Or laughing at our own attempts to be helpful, knowing we're imperfect and fallible."

"Yes."

A long silence followed, and Brand finally spoke up.

"Now I'm going to tell you a story. Not one with such a happy ending. Did you read about the recent shooting in Dallas? Five white police officers were killed and another seven wounded by a former Army sniper."

"Yes. The story I read said he was targeting them in retaliation for recent police shootings of unarmed black men in Minnesota and Louisiana."

"Well, I was there."

"Oh my, what happened?"

"It was an ambush. That's what is so unfathomable. The realization, not in war but peace, that the claw of death is reaching for you ..."

The chaplain heard something in his friend's voice that was very different from previous talks. It was fearful and unsure.

"How did you happen to be in Dallas? And at the march?"

"I was visiting friends, a solo trip. My wife remained back east. When the news about the shootings in Minnesota and Louisiana first broke, people began planning protest events. I got a call from a friend who is a rabbi, a community leader there in Dallas. He was planning to march with a Black Lives Matter group. He said, 'It will be peaceful. Will you come?'

"I was hesitant, partly because of my military rank and obligations. But I took some time to pray and decided I would lock arms with the people of Dallas.

"It was dark by the time we began. People from all walks marched and my friend was right, the whole thing was peaceful. I fell into conversation with strangers who expressed fear and anger over the deaths in Louisiana and Minnesota. When I could

I consoled, but mostly I listened. I liked the sound of all the voices—but then, out of nowhere, gunfire began.

"By then we were downtown, where city blocks make it feel like you're walking through valleys. The collision of bodies, the panic, were suffocating. It felt like powerful cross-currents of water. I couldn't keep my balance. I fell and was trampled until I was pulled up by the rabbi and another man."

"Were you injured?"

"No, but we were trapped and felt like we could die at any moment. We couldn't tell the location of the shooter or shooters. It made me feel like I was being stalked, but for what reason?"

"My God, of course, you were so vulnerable."

"Yes. You know what it's like. You've been through some fire-fights in Iraq."

"The danger. You breathe it."

"Yeah, it burns your lungs. But this…this was more terrifying than anything I've experienced before. The mass of people made it impossible for me to even attempt escape. And… and that's when I lost it."

The chaplain respected the silence by holding his breath, waiting for whatever his mentor was willing to share.

"I didn't want to die. I'd just become a grandfather and been promoted to a rank I had thought impossible for me to achieve when I was younger. I had coveted being in Washington, as a person of some … prominence?

"Yet everything I'd learned and shared with others, all the confidence, the so-called wisdom about God's plan … I crumbled and cried. Like everyone else walking peacefully on that fine Dallas night. Yet I stopped … believing. Does this sound familiar?"

"Familiar?"

"Think about our discourse."

"The attainments?"

"*Think.*"

It took a moment. But then it came to him and the chaplain was certain of his answer. "The third attainment."

"How so?"

"God's ultimate plan for hurt and pain."

"Good. Yes. God's Providence. And belief in it is challenging when we feel buried by tragedy, accidents, and stupidity."

"You were ambushed, Sir."

"That's kind. Thank you."

Brand seemed so distant now, like his mind was still in Dallas. Finally, he returned with a question.

"Do you know what saved me?"

"Please, I want to know."

"After pulverizing the third attainment, I berated myself—still surrounded by living hell. Then I got back to basics. I climbed down the ladder and started all over. At the bottom rung, I spoke. 'I am powerless.'"

"Out loud?"

"You bet. And others heard me despite all the noise. I was in civilian clothes, so they had no idea who I was. I got some odd looks, but I said it again."

"I am powerless."

"Yes. And a young woman took my hand and repeated: *I am powerless*"

Col. Brand described how others joined in and held hands until the small group became a choir, resonating, proclaiming, despite the danger. A pulsation could be felt. It gathered strength, an electrical current, that lifted their voices until …

Another burst of automated gunfire sent them diving for cover. Crawling on his belly to a trash receptacle, repeating his I am powerless mantra, Brand propped himself up and looked for his friend, the rabbi. No luck.

"Then I tried to guess which direction we had we come from. Nothing looked familiar. So in my frustration can you guess what I said?"

"I am not God!" The chaplain was emphatic.

"Yes. It gave me a lift. I couldn't stop the shooting. Or the terror. I might not survive. But I could relieve myself of that burden. The burden of thinking it was up to me to make everything better, immediately."

"So how did you get out of there, Sir?"

"A little boy."

"What?"

"He saw me and seemed concerned, like I was his grandpa. He came to me and asked if I'd seen his mother. His cheeks were stained with tears. I took his hand and followed him down Main Street, until we found others who were sheltered."

"Did you think you were spared because of Providence?"

The pause was long. "I've always felt like God had a protective hand on my life. After I reconnected with my friend, we heard police officers were the targets, not us. Even so I know we could have been killed."

"Were you aware then that the shooter was an Army vet who had been in Afghanistan?"

"When I heard the shooter was ex-military, lots of questions bounced through my head.

Had he spent time with a chaplain? And if so, how did we lose him? Could we have helped him through his trauma, his decision to kill?"

"Maybe. Maybe not."

"My friend and I decided we should go to the hospital to assist, if we could. Some police were near the emergency room, grown men and women, strong people who were shattered to hear that friends and colleagues were dead. To see our protectors so weakened … and to see doctors and nurses, our healers, emotionally exhausted … it made me shudder. Our foundation was under assault. We were all, in our own way, trying desperately to … to …"

"To cope."

"Yes. I'd thought, after all I'd experienced as a chaplain, that I had a handle on things.

Dallas humbled me deeply. It destroyed my faith and then, returned it. I stayed on for a few days to be part of the mourning, the grief."

"To help the healing begin."

"Hold on there, partner. That takes time. Even when you think the healing has happened, other people's pain triggers memories, things we wish we were able to forget.

"But," Brand continued, "Sometimes we forget there is such a thing as post-traumatic growth. Bad things might help make us better people."

"Chaplain Brand ... thank you."

"Hm. I was about to thank *you*."

"For what?"

"For your ministry. For listening so well."

13

THE FOURTH ATTAINMENT

SELF-CARE

COPING WITH POWERLESSNESS IS NOT ALWAYS CONSCIOUS. CHAPLAIN Parker broke into uncontrollable laughter after an exhausting, tragic day. He did not open a Caregiver's Toolbox and carefully choose an instrument he felt was appropriate. His laughter was spontaneous, an unconscious relief of tension, not an objective or rational choice.

Yet many of the chaplains interviewed for this book developed intentional methods to help them cope with the overwhelming and unpredictable nature of powerlessness. The term most often used when describing their insights was *self-care*.

Mastering self-care means the caregiver understands when they need to step back and be mindful of their own needs. One chaplain put it this way: "I need to recharge my batteries and have some downtime. I take care of myself so that I can take care of others."

The methods chaplains favor when coping with powerlessness can be divided into four areas of concern: **physical, spiritual, social, mental**.

One chaplain said his feelings of powerlessness often yielded after working out at the gym. "I remember one day when my mind was screaming after processing so many problems. I thought I would never get to sleep that night, but after a long workout, I was so physically exhausted that I slept well. The next day I was refreshed and able to focus again."

Another told him, "I got a call notifying me that a long-time friend had been killed in Afghanistan. I left my office and went straight to a park where I run sometimes. I changed into my gym clothes and started running. I ran until it got too dark to continue. I don't know how long I ran, but it was long enough to help me shake some of the pain I was feeling."

Maintaining spiritual discipline was the coping method most often mentioned by chaplains. Several described how prayer and Bible study helped them deal with stress. "There's something soothing about reading the Scriptures," said a Baptist chaplain from Georgia. "It helps me when I read the Psalms and see David crying out to God in his pain. Whenever I take my problems to God like that, the burden always lifts from me."

Turning to God and reading Scripture, in other words, is much like physical exertion: it must be done often to tone the mind and give a sense of purpose. The chaplains interviewed made these remarks about the value of spiritual disciplines:

- "I realized, again, that I wasn't alone. Giving it to God was humbling and a big relief."
- "Turning to God when experiencing powerlessness replenishes me."
- "Reading Scripture encourages me to carry on. I feel embraced, and this inspires me to rely on and believe in the simple act of praying."

Getting to God, feeling His presence, is the true purpose of these caregiver disciplines because powerlessness is sure to find us when we are disconnected. When we think, "I am God," and then fail to deliver His wisdom and healing power, we are ripe for a downfall. By giving their burdens to God, they re-establish a source of comfort that only He provides.

Long ago, Chaplain Parker recognized the value of sharing his problems with trusted colleagues and friends. He purposefully sought counsel from his supervisor, Col. Brand.

When Parker mentioned this to one colleague, the officer quipped, "Oh, is he your higher power?"

The chaplain laughed, then paused a moment to reply.

"Yes, in the context of rank and responsibility, he is. I now recognize how much a skilled and compassionate leader can say and do to lift a burden from our shoulders. He's not taking the place of God, but I've found that social interaction is an essential mode of coping. Staying silent and remote is counterproductive."

Interviews with chaplains showed that those who relied on peers and mentors to talk through their difficulties saw great value in processing, intellectually and emotionally, the complex and sometimes disturbing scenarios that confronted them at war and at home.

These comments from interviews affirm the importance of self-care.

- "Mentors are a huge resource. They've been doing this longer; they are more experienced and can be trusted. I can't underestimate their role during deployment."
- "We need care, and often that means having someone to talk to. Without that outlet, we burn out quickly, and our ministry becomes meaningless."
- "I become a miserable person who can be of no help to anyone. That's why self-care methods must be practiced on a regular basis."
- "Chaplains and all caregivers must seek out people that are knowledgeable. Ask them questions, learn from them."
- "Being a caregiver is a team sport."

The chaplains said the mental aspect of coping well demands

skill development. One described it as getting a superior toolbox that contains more options for getting the job done. Ironically, by studying and learning more about human beings, chaplains begin to feel more powerful, and yet do not succumb to the fool's errand of believing "I am God." In short, like professionals in other walks of life, they develop confidence in their ability to assist in times of crisis.

One essential skill mentioned was learning to make referrals. If you don't have the skill-set required to help a soldier in distress, make what contribution you can, and then refer the soldier, colleague or patient to an expert who can help resolve the troubling issue.

This might seem humbling, an admission by a chaplain that he or she lacks specific skills. But this is how one veteran chaplain explained this referral skill and the importance of expanding experience and expertise:

"You get used to doing ministry in a traumatic event where it's not about me, it's about the person to whom I'm ministering. One thing that helped me get over myself was a two-week emergency medical ministry course at Brooke Army Medical Center.[1] I worked in the trauma ward, learning to get used to suffering without being desensitized to it. I wasn't a doctor, but I knew I could contribute."

Capt. Parker recognized how valuable the discussions with his mentor were in helping him see the bigger picture. Understanding his limitations and in good conscience making referrals is a more efficient way to help people overcome mental or physical demons. He remembered another thing Brand said, "The caregiver who avoids ego and only wants to contribute is growing. Don't fret over what you can't do. Be proud of what you can do. And know that by relying on colleagues, leaders, etc., you can still play an important role."

Parker began to think about how he could learn to improve his level of care. Suddenly a smile crossed his face. *Laughing and crying are not learned skills. We can't develop them, we can only surrender to them. But what power they have.* He thought of his outburst of laughter with the Jeffersons. And the heart cry of Chaplain Brand when he talked about his experience in Dallas.

That conversation was a turning point in their relationship. He shouldn't have been surprised then by the senior officer's appreciation of his role as a listener and friend.

Brand called the next week and invited him to Washington for a couple days. "I'd be honored, Sir. Do you think leadership will approve?"

"I'm in charge around here. Pack your bags, my friend."

------

1. Brooke Army Medical Center (BAMC) is the United States Army's premier medical institution. Located in San Antonio, BAMC is the Army's largest and busiest medical facility.

14

COMBAT READINESS

PREPARING FOR THE SPIRITUAL BATTLE

Colonel Brand was waiting when Tim Parker deplaned on the tarmac at Joint Base Andrews. He smiled and extended his hand, "Welcome back to DC, Tim."

"Thanks. It feels like coming home."

"Good. You'll be staying at my home tonight, but first, let's go get some dinner." He pointed to a black Jeep Cherokee parked nearby, and soon they were out the front gate.

"Food's good at the Officers' Club, but you can choose."

Capt. Parker thought a moment. "My wife and I used to eat at an Applebee's near my old office. How's that sound?"

"Let's do it."

Forty-five minutes later, they were feasting on steak and salad. "I brought you here because I'm concerned about you."

Parker looked stunned. "Have I messed up on something?"

"No, not at all. You're a first-rate chaplain. Wise. Caring. Deeply committed to the people you serve. My concern is for you personally. That you need to work on your physical and spiritual disciplines. That you need to unburden yourself of stuff you should rightfully entrust to God and other chaplains."

"Does this have something to do with the attainments?"

"Yes, you're doing a lot of things right, especially the way you process issues with me and other chaplains. You work hard at improving your skills. But are you working just as hard to stay fit physically and spiritually?"

"I'm not sure what you mean."

"A good chaplain is a soldier preparing for battle, only on a deeper level. You must get the exercise and rest you need to stay strong physically and mentally. Then there's the spiritual side of it. What are you doing to be battle ready?"

"I like to play racquetball. Good cardio. But I've been kind of sporadic with exercise lately. Not sleeping so well either. The cases we handle get to me sometimes."

Col. Brand locked eyes with his younger friend. "You can't let this be an optional part of your life. Make it a priority. Every day."

"OK. Battle ready." Parker stared down at the last of his salad and stirred it nervously with his fork.

"Getting ready spiritually is even more important. I love the way you devour books, and your understanding of Scripture is excellent. But are you taking time to meditate, to listen?"

The younger chaplain again looked confused.

"By that, I mean quiet time. Lots of pastors read the Bible and pray in their personal devotions. But not so many take time to meditate on what they've read or to listen for answers to the things they've just prayed. The Catholics have a better understanding of this than a lot of us Protestants," Brand said. "They do silent retreats so they can quiet their spirits and listen to what God may have to say to them."

"Hmmm. I pray a lot, but I do all the talking. So how does that work? I mean how do you recognize God's voice?"

"Well, in my experience, something pops into my mind. Sometimes it's a Scripture verse that speaks directly to what I've been praying about. Sometimes it's a name. And when I call that person, it becomes abundantly clear the prompt was from God. Other times, I simply feel peace. Like God is saying, 'Yes, I'll take that burden from you.'"

"I guess I still have a lot to learn about prayer."

"The other thing I want you to learn is your own limitations. As chaplains, we don't have to take every case that walks through our office door. But I see you trying to help everybody."

Chaplain Parker flashed a look that said without words, 'Guilty as charged.'

"I'm sure you recognize that just as the Army has specialists in various kinds of weapons, we chaplains develop our own specialties. You have a gift for dealing with marriage and family issues. Other chaplains work well on substance abuse counselling or PTSD cases or handling personnel conflicts.

"What I'm suggesting, Tim, is that you make referrals to Army specialists with advanced degrees and certifications— generally not something a chaplain would cover. Those colleagues are better skilled in handling these cases. That's no reflection on you. It's wise leadership. And good self-care."

"That's what this conversation is all about, isn't it? Good self-care."

"Yes, it is. I don't want to see you burn out and drop out. You're too good an officer to let that happen."

Parker felt a lump in his throat. What he thought was a reprimand of sorts had become perhaps the best affirmation he'd ever received.

"Sir, I don't understand why you've invested so much time in me. But I am deeply grateful. I want to be the best soldier, the best chaplain I can be."

"There's another reason I brought you here. We have a loaded C-17 coming in tomorrow, and I can use an experienced greeter like you to help me."

"Anything you need, Sir … And not only tomorrow. Call me anytime."

15

WHEN WILL IT END?

GRIMM MISSION RESCUE

THE CHAPLAINS WATCHED IN AWE AS THE MASSIVE C-17 Globemaster dropped below the cloud layer at Joint Base Andrews near Washington, D.C. A winter wind was coming in off the North Atlantic, so they stood in the shelter of buses and medical vehicles operated by the welcoming team of physicians and nurses.

This time there was no small talk among the caregivers. They had been notified that the flight was at capacity. With so many wounded warriors on the plane, each with a different type of injury or set of orders, the caregivers' transitioning work would be complex.

Parker did not recognize any names on the synopsis list. There would be no uncomfortable reunions so he could take each case as it came. Yet something nagged at him, and Col. Brand noticed.

"Everything all right?"

"Yes, Sir, yes. It's just …"

"Go on."

"When will these planes stop flying? I mean, they're remarkable."

"I'm amazed every time I see one of these magnificent birds."

"Yes, they're like airborne hospitals. Awesome to behold."

"I always hear 'but' in your comments." He was grinning.

Tim Parker nodded a mea culpa. "*But* ... when will we no longer need to bring broken people back home?"

Now Col. Brand hesitated. "When will war end, is that the question?"

"The killing. The ..."

"Trauma."

"Broken soldiers and shattered families. Gold Star families. I love them for their sacrifice, but I wish there were no such thing. I wish Gold Star meant exemplary or commendable or ..."

"Well, of course, it does mean that. Exemplary as a synonym for the ultimate sacrifice, the giving of a son or daughter to the jaws of hell. But I share your unrest. It's like a Brothers Grimm tale. To stop the wicked witch and evil ogre, we feed them our best and brightest. We want a happy ending. We want to liberate ourselves from whatever evil continues to stalk us. Right?"

"Yeah ..."

The powerful plane touched down, and its screeching brakes stole their attention for a moment. Its velocity and thrust slowed, and the aircraft taxied toward the welcoming team.

Once on the bus Brand picked up the conversation.

"Let's say it will never end. The wicked witch, Satan, or whatever evil is in control keeps this horrible nightmare going."

"A Grimm, dreadful thought, but go on."

"A fairy tale offers a principle, or perhaps some kind of moral or paradox. You're trying to get to the moral of this story."

"Sir, the thing is, what if the war goes on and on but the people, people like us, grow too weary to do what we do? What if nobody wants this job anymore because the haunted forest goes on and on and ..."

Their bus lurched forward, joining the procession of medical vehicles, yet the chaplain continued, though he was drawing some curious stares from the medical workers across the aisle.

"If the wounded warrior planes keep coming then the care-givers will be there too."

"They have to show up."

"But will they?"

When the bus stopped, they stood and waited their turn to disembark. The chaplain now felt some tension between him and Colonel Brand. They had work to do, but he yearned for a fuller response from his advisor. They stepped off the vehicle as the rear hatch of the C-17 opened and physicians and nurses swept into the plane.

Brand broke the silence again. "You see, this is where we rely on the Brothers Grimm. Yes, there is evil in that forest, and yes there are many tales where suffering lasts what seems like an eternity, until …"

Now the chaplains were moving too. Once on board, they began their walk down the center aisle, nodding at men and women, some of whom looked frightened whereas others were medicated so heavily their eyes revealed nothing but a fog.

"Full capacity today, my friend," Brand said softly.

"Yes. Yes. We'll be here awhile. So what were you going to say? 'Suffering lasts an eternity, until …'"

"Yes. Right. Well … *until* a hero appears, seemingly from nowhere. Young, resourceful, unabashed. Even foolish at times but quick, clever. Best of all, *willing*. That's what I love about fairy tales, there is always an opposite force, dormant but ready to be unleashed."

Brand put a hand on the chaplain's shoulder and smiled. "Shall we get started?"

———

THE SHOUTING BEGAN MINUTES LATER. The chaplains stepped aside as physicians rushed to help a Marine whose condition had rapidly deteriorated. A nurse called out, "We're losing him."

How many times have I had heard those words, on the battlefield, in hospitals? Parker thought.

The Marine's wife, who had traveled on the plane with her husband, kept silent, but her face was an open wound.

Brand went to her and, without a word, took her in his arms and helped her follow the gurney into a waiting ambulance. That's when her emotions burst.

"We were almost home. Oh God, we were almost home!"

Chaplain Parker's heart began to tremble. Watching someone die always shook him emotionally. He knew he was vulnerable to doubt and depression in such situations. He quickly reminded himself of good advice he got from Chaplain Brand: *Understand the triggers and acknowledge them. Recognize that working through these painful situations can make you a better caregiver.*

He moved farther down the center aisle, reaching out, sometimes only holding a hand or whispering encouragement. He was conscious of the intimacy, the shared fears, and minor miracles, but lost track of time or his own needs. Amputees, infantrymen with head wounds, and shell-shocked PTSD cases surrounded the most curious demographic of the wounded—the smilers. They were just happy to be alive, no matter how severe their wounds. Capt. Parker noticed one smiler sitting upright, his neck supported in a brace.

"That looks uncomfortable."

The young soldier couldn't shrug, so he flashed a grin. "No worries. It feels like a necktie. I never did like dressing up."

"Not even for the high school prom?"

"I went in my jeans and drove my daddy's pickup. They wouldn't let me in."

"Didn't like your wardrobe?"

"Didn't have a date. Heartbreak is worse than any broken neck, I'll tell you that, Chaplain."

Oklahoma—a hint of it—was in his voice. His body-type shouted rodeo. Details. Biographies. This was what the chaplain loved so much about his path. A greeting, and then jokes, queries, revelations.

"So how did you get injured?"

"I rolled off a bridge."

"Why'd you do that?"

"Well, you know, I was in a vehicle."

"Oh, right."

"Dang car got all torn to bits, but not Mr. Prom King. How come?"

Pointing to the brace, "Well, hey, I'd say you've suffered a little collateral damage."

"Yeah, but, man, I shouldn't be sitting here. Know what I'm saying? I should be looking up at the stars as they lower me into my grave. *I tell you.*"

The wonder of it all glowed in his face. But gratitude, as well. He described how he'd crawled out of the wreckage and was found by medics on his back, unconscious, under a brutal, hot sun.

"God spared me, Chaplain. Will you help me give my thanks, I mean, you know, properly?"

"Properly?" he teased. "Jeans and cowboy boots are as good as a tux when giving praise."

"Yeah, OK, but I hope He'll understand if I don't bow my head."

Laughs before a prayer: Double blessings.

———

AFTER GREETING MORE WOUNDED WARRIORS, Parker caught the eye of a nurse who nodded toward the soldier seated near the front of the aircraft. "She won't budge. This plane needs to move on. I don't want to have to strap her to a gurney. Maybe you can get her going."

The chaplain approached a soldier, who seemed lost in

thought. Her trim, long body swam in the camouflage uniform and combat boots; a blunt cut kept her straight black hair from touching her shoulders. She was still strapped in, the safety harness pinning her back to the interior wall of the plane.

He looked at his list of passengers and found the name Kronig, which was on her nameplate.

"Giang? Giang Kronig?" She looked up.

"How we doing?"

"We?"

Her gaze was piercing though not angry.

"Sorry. How are *you* doing?"

She looked away and shook her head. "I'm not leaving."

"But most of the other passengers ..."

"The other passengers had no choice, most of them."

She was right. Without complaint, the injured were wheeled out of the belly of the gray goose that had brought them stateside. They were now headed to hospitals or boarding the next flight to wherever they'd been assigned.

"You know the command is going to taxi this plane to maintenance, get it ready for its next flight."

"Sounds good."

"They need to empty the plane before ..."

"They can sweep around me. I'm going back."

"Back to Germany?"

"I'll start there, then make it back to my company."

"In Iraq?"

"Yes, Sir."

That wasn't possible, of course. The synopsis on Giang Kronig said she had been sent home for a Veterans Administration medical review. The outcome would determine if she could remain in the military.

"So you don't want to meet with the VA?"

"I already know what they're going to say."

"And what's that?"

"I'm done. They won't let me serve anymore."

These VA board reviews determined the future of many soldiers coming from battle zones. Clearly, Kronig had her mind set on staying in the Army.

The chaplain sat next to her, took a deep breath. "Mind if I wait with you?"

"Wait?"

"Sooner or later they'll have to drag you out."

A long silence followed, and tears appeared in her eyes. "No. I can't let them down."

"Who?"

"My family. We've fought for this country since the American Revolution. I enlisted, and my children will enlist. No matter what the VA says, "I know my body. I can serve."

The chaplain backed off, remembering that it was not his job to make a soldier agree. He used to feel rewarded when men and women took his advice. He'd learned, though, that all he was seeking was approval, so he weaned himself from the need to hear some form of "yes." In doing so, he discovered that going in the opposite direction brought more meaningful conversations.

"So your family would respect you, if you were carried off this plane for disobeying an order, right?"

"No! I don't want to disappoint my family!"

"Because you're a daughter of the American Revolution?" She nodded.

"So tell me about that. I'd like to learn more about your life."

Her father had served in Vietnam where he met Giang's mother. Pregnant, she was airlifted to safety when Saigon was captured by Viet Cong. Giang was born in San Diego, became a high school track star, but her most significant goal was to extend the family's military lineage.

"Daddy's family, his whole family served. I can't stop now. This is my life."

He realized her struggle was like that of Matt Kennedy, Tally Grimes, and Deshawn Jefferson—distress about impending change.

"Loss, loss, loss, right? That's what you're feeling."

"Yes."

"It all seems so unfair to someone like you who has dedicated her life to the service. I can understand why you don't want to leave the plane."

He let the silence prevail. "I'll stay with you."

"No. You'll get in trouble."

"Let 'em drag us both out of here. You kick, and I'll scream."

She protested with a laugh. "No!"

"Well, then, let's consider our options."

"*Our* options?" This time the challenge was friendly.

The chaplain carefully summarized her dilemma, contrasting her stubbornness and fear of loss with her obvious respect for family and tradition.

"If you stay here, strapped to the aircraft," he smiled before continuing, "you'll get your life back, right?"

The gloom returned. "No."

"But by facing the VA review, like a soldier, the very least you'll do is make your father and mother proud, right?"

She exhaled and grit her teeth as if biting the hard nail of acceptance. "Yes."

A moment later, Giang unlatched her safety harness and stood, turning toward the gaping exit, where she could see the tarmac and a man with silver hair in an Army officer's uniform. He stood still, composed, and he was smiling.

"Who's that?" she asked.

"Col. Robert Brand. He's also a chaplain."

"He looks kind."

"Yes, he is. And wise too. Want to meet him? He's a *lifer*, like you."

They processed down the center of the aircraft in silence, but when they reached the ramp Giang stopped.

"What will I do next?"

"I don't know, Giang."

"Neither do I—obviously. But I have faith. God is in control, right?"

"That's right."

"He'll bring me somewhere that's even better. Something I might never have thought of." Then she saluted and hurried off the plane, ready to test her fate.

16

THE FIFTH ATTAINMENT

I AM CHANGED

"Am I vain to think I'm changed, that I'm a better chaplain than I was when we first met?"

COL. BRAND LEANED BACK IN HIS SOFT OFFICE CHAIR, PARTIALLY IN shadow due to the dimming light of the Sabbath.

He smiled. "'Vanity thy name is …' chaplain? No. If we're willing to do the hard work of self-examination, then we're entitled to acknowledge growth. And you have grown, Tim. I was quite taken with the ease you showed today on the plane, working with so many different people."

"Thank you."

"It's a maturation process, isn't it? Chaplains and other caregivers begin to express an increased sense of maturity, or a 'mature faith,' as a colleague once called it."

Parker nodded. He recognized now he was more likely to relax into conversations with returning soldiers and not feel like it was his job to cure an illness or fix a problem. That felt like progress. He also felt far more skilled at resolving feelings of powerlessness before they paralyzed his consciousness. He could trace this transformation to adjustments he'd made as his mentor defined the first four attainments.

"I understand now that caregivers don't finally overcome powerlessness. The feeling comes back. But it doesn't have to crush us." He thought of his mentor's unflinching candor about the ambush in Dallas. It was a reminder that at any time even a veteran can be humbled.

Col. Brand leaned forward, "Change, in other words, is a community process, peer-to-peer, and mentor-to-protégé, delivered on the backs of three simple truths:

"You can't force transformation, it's not something you can dictate. Caregivers change when they acknowledge feelings of powerlessness and accept that they can't fix everything. And finally, the attainments illuminate a path that involves trusting God—or some higher power— with the outcome. It's still a choice to follow that path."

"I've talked to quite a few colleagues about how they deal with powerlessness," said Tim Parker. "One guy told me, 'It is a maturing *thought* process. The more you walk with the Lord, the more you grow in faith. It's the faith that keeps us from being paralyzed by powerlessness.' Another guy had a practical but less spiritual insight. He said: 'Life is a tension between two opposite things, pushing and pulling. It can only be resolved by doing what you deem to be in the best interest of the person you are counseling. We must pick the wisest path between two forces. Find that sweet spot.'"

Brand laughed, "Yes, I've done that a few times. It didn't always work out so well. We all deal every single day with things we have no control over. A maturity born of faith and wisdom makes the difference,"

"Yes, spiritual maturity," Parker said. "And like you said before, that includes a mature view of my pastoral identity. I have to remind myself that my identity is not in my job, but in Christ. We are His instruments."

"Caring for soldiers is noble work," Col. Brand said. "Respect its value. The changed acknowledges the worth of something as simple as listening, while the powerless chaplain says things like, 'The only thing I can do is listen when what I really want is to fix everything.'"

"I do appreciate this work, much more so since I've been dialoguing with you, Sir."

"The mature chaplain recognizes that being present, as God's incarnate representative, dilutes anxiety in the people we serve. We cannot stop all of life's tragic events from happening. We can accept that God is always at work, whether we like the circumstances or not."

"Not every chaplain trusts that."

"True. Especially during an episode of powerlessness. But that's my point. The irony is that the only means of escape from that dreaded experience is to believe in something bigger than ourselves. 'I am changed' reflects how chaplains perceive the Divine and their ministry."

Chaplain Parker nodded, then deep in thought, his eyes drifted across the many books in his mentor's office.

"Or, consider Honest Abe's way of describing the process." Brand opened a small book, read it aloud, and handed it to his protégé."

"I have been driven many times upon my knees by the overwhelming conviction that I had nowhere else to go. My own wisdom and that of all about me seemed insufficient for that day."

— —ABRAHAM LINCOLN

"Good quote," Parker said as he took out his iPhone and made a note of the title and page number."

"I think old Abe recognized that we too often try to solve everything in our own wisdom and strength, but it's in weakness that we open our hearts and minds to the power of God."

"I can't stop thinking about all the people I've met. In some ways, I want to know what happened to them. Are they safe and happy? But sometimes I don't want to know. That's when I begin to feel anxious, fearful that things have not worked out for them."

"Like who?"

"Sgt. Matt Kennedy. I was in Iraq with him when he lost a friend. Then we met last time I was here in Washington. His family, his kids …I just want him to be …"

"Wanting won't make it so."

"But …"

Brand chuckled. "There's that word again."

The chaplain blushed.

"You see, we catch ourselves, don't we, falling back into our need to resolve someone else's despair. To make things better. You gave what you could."

"True."

"And even if his pressing issues have resolved pleasingly, something else might be troubling him now."

The chaplain's mind then went to Daniel Roth, who had grieved so deeply for his deceased comrade and lover. And Clara, the seventeen-year-old mother who was raising an out-of-wedlock child. And his friend Tally Grimes, now out of the Army and working as a pastor.

"Call them up," Brand suggested. "These days it is not so hard to find people."

"Yeah, well, that's the other part of it. I feel I would be intruding.

"You're not intruding. You're being a good pastor."

"I would like to follow up with a soldier we met today. Giang. It doesn't look good for her. The decision is not hers."

"She must accept the board's ruling."

"And it doesn't look good."

"These words we use, *good, bad,* what do they mean? Giang will have other choices to make, or she'll be led to something new. That's her story."

"Her fairy tale?"

"Well, not all things in life can be explained or completely understood. But if we could see our lives as stories that will, in some way, benefit others …"

Brand didn't finish the thought.

Nor did the chaplain, because he couldn't. He was tired and resigned to the fact that he'd have to live with the questions, the nagging anxieties. He had a plane to catch in the morning and a new deployment to face in only a few weeks.

"I'm so grateful for all this time you've given me, Sir." "It's been my pleasure. Let's get some rest."

Nearly a year after his visit with Col. Brand in Washington, D.C., the chaplain was scrolling through his email when a subject line caught his eye: *Warrior Rebound.*

Giang Kronig had indeed been discharged from military service and, initially, she admitted that it felt as though she were recovering from major surgery. Severed from her military family the days were formless and the nights, way too long.

…Then one night I woke up and thought, stop feeling sorry for yourself. I realized that other soldiers just like me needed help adjusting. And, hey, is the Veterans Administration capable of handling all these transitions? No.

Suddenly a door opened, and I saw my future. I had found a new way to serve.

The next day I began raising money for my start-up called *Warrior Entrepreneur.* I've convinced counselors, therapists and business experts to share resources and even jobs, in some cases. We'll retrain veterans to live well—after serving so proudly.

Thank you for listening that day on the plane in DC.

You helped more than you know.

Giang Kronig

He returned her email, praising her effort and offering to help in any way that he could.

Then he dialed his phone. Brand picked up on the first ring. "Hello, Tim. How are you?"

"Hello to you too, Sir. I'm well. I'm sure you're busy, but I had to tell you. Remember all our talk about fairy tales and the evolving theory and all that?"

"Of course."

"Well, if you have a minute, I'd like to share a happy ending."

"Ending?"

The question caused Chaplain Tim to pause and reconsider how he should share Giang's story.

"Actually, it's a happy beginning."

AFTERWORD

INTERVIEW YOURSELF

How strange to think the people who come to our aid during a crisis may not value their contribution to our lives. Yet when chaplains and other caregivers experience powerlessness, many lose faith in their gift to society.

This book was written to show these men and women that accepting powerlessness is a necessary first step in the process of transformation. In working through the Five Attainments, a new perspective should emerge—and with it, an improved sense of identity that deepens their devotion to their calling of service.

Let's not pretend this change is effortless. First, the individual must contend with personal pride and ego, which often flares up when we put too much emphasis on achievement. As chaplains, we must follow the example of Jesus humbling Himself on the cross. Despite having the power to stop His sacrifice, He accepted it, so the will of the Father could be fulfilled. As a result, He was given the highest position in the Kingdom.

Amid death and destruction, on the home front and overseas, we are called to live a life of love and compassion and service.

In the military, our battle strategists often use the expression, "The enemy has a vote." This means our officers may plot out certain objectives, but recognize the "good guys" cannot always carry them out. The enemy may surprise or overwhelm them. Or some other traumatic event may occur despite their best-laid plans. This expression allows leaders to acknowledge they are not God. They do, however, have a vote. The choices they make affect the outcome.

So it is with many caregivers. Throughout my interviews, various chaplains described this moment of truth. They could surrender to the paralysis that happens after unsuccessful attempts to stop war, or heal every injured person, or vanquish everyone's fear. Or, the chaplains could accept their finiteness and allow the power, grace, and presence of God to be shown through them.

This decision becomes a wrestling match that, in some ways, is characterized by the story of Jacob fighting with God on the bank of the Jabbok River (Gen. 32: 22-31). In the end, those who have grappled with God and won are changed persons. Their self-defeating burden to control everything is lifted. As one participant stated, "I had to either stay stuck in the mud or pull myself out and get over myself." Like Jacob, this chaplain cast his vote and won his wrestling match by being transformed.

Another way to vote is to seek relationships with peers, mentors, and God to process their experiences. Creating a support group, a community, is a valuable coping mechanism. Through these relationships, caregivers resolve feelings of powerlessness.

Not every caregiver is crushed by powerlessness. In my quest to illuminate this issue, I met chaplains who understood they could not change anyone. I asked if they were being completely honest with themselves, and even when pressed, their mindset and theology would not allow them to get caught up trying to fix things. They understood the limits of their ministry and didn't exceed them. One chaplain said he doesn't get personally involved, "Because I know God is involved."

I struggled with this response. Remaining detached, refusing to show more compassion for a soldier's problems, initially struck me as crass. The equivalent of requesting help from a bureaucrat only to hear the apathetic response, "Sorry, it's not my job."

However, I had to look within and realize that my judgment of another chaplain's attitude might lead to the egotistic dead-end of trying to fix things. Accepting personal limits was precisely how we avoid futility and deflect the trap of powerlessness. It was a realistic and mature decision that some caregivers grasp sooner than others.

One chaplain came to his conclusion after recognizing parallels between supporting his commander and serving God. He said, "It finally sunk in that Army commanders are given authority to make decisions and that my authority was limited by clear-cut guidance from my superiors. This helped me to disengage when trying to help a soldier. Yes, I'm a participant, I can make recommendations to the commander, but it was useless to try to persuade him to accept my view. I'm not the commander, and I'm not God."

The transformation needed to address powerlessness comes in part from accepting authority (God's and man's) and changing in ourselves what needs to change. Each day, in Twelve Step groups around the world, millions recite a simple mantra called the Serenity Prayer:

> God grant me the serenity to accept the things I
> cannot change, the courage to change the
> things I can, and the wisdom to know the
> difference.

Change, or the need for change, is a constant and is not to be feared.

A simple way to personally explore the issues dramatized in *A Chaplain's Battle* is to ask the questions I asked my colleagues. In each interview, I started with a focus on powerlessness (see below). Follow-up questions led to discussions about how then to deal with it.

- Can you describe a situation in which you felt powerless during a deployment?
- What makes you feel powerless?

- What other types of situations can you think of that made you felt helpless or powerless?
- How often do you have situations in which you feel powerless?
- What is the effect on you, having feelings of powerlessness?
- How do you resolve the feelings of powerlessness then?
- How relevant is powerlessness in your life?
- Is there anything I haven't asked about your experiences that you believe might be crucial?

Chaplains and other caregivers today come from various religious backgrounds. So do The Five Attainments apply only to those with a spiritual perspective? Not at all.

Powerlessness has a way of bringing people—religious and non-religious—to their knees. The best caregivers have themselves experienced brokenness and helplessness. Their compassion and faithfulness make them uniquely qualified to point the way to healing.

BIBLIOGRAPHY

Cadge, W., & Catlin, W. A. (2006). Making sense of suffering and death: How health care providers construct meanings in a neonatal intensive care unit. *Journal of Religion and Health, 45(2)*, 248-263.

Coyle, N., & Ferrell, B. R. (2008). The nature of suffering and the goals of nursing.
Oncology Nursing Forum, 35(2), 241-253.

Demacopoulos, G. (2007). *St. Gregory the Great: The Book of Pastoral Rule*. Crestwood, NY: St. Vladimir's Seminary Press.

Dyslin, C. W. (2008). The power of powerlessness: The role of spiritual surrender and interpersonal confession in the treatment of addictions. *Journal of Psychology and Christianity, 27(1)*, 41-55.

Gerkin, C. (1979). *Crisis Experience in Modern Life: Theory and Theology for Pastoral Care*.
Nashville: Abingdon Press.

Gerkin, C. (1980). Power and powerlessness in clinical pastoral education. *Journal of Pastoral Care, 34(2)*, 114-124.

Glaser, B. G., & Strauss, A. L., (1967). *The Discovery of Grounded Theory: Strategies for Qualitative Research*. Chicago: Aldine Pub.

Heldebrand, J., & Markovic, D. (2007). Systemic therapists' experience of powerlessness. *ANZJFT, 28(4)*, 191-199.

Kornhaber, R. A., & Wilson, A., (2011). Enduring feelings of powerlessness as a burns nurse: A descriptive phenomenological inquiry. *Contemporary Nurse, 39(2)*, 172-179.

McClelland, D., (1975). *Power: The inner experience*. NYC: Irvington Publishers.

McGrath-Merkle, C., (2010). Gregory the Great's Metaphor of the Physician of the Heart
    as a Model for Pastoral Identity. *Journal of Religion and Health, 50*(2), 374-388.

Oden, T. C., & Browning, D. S., (1984). *Care of Souls in the Classic Tradition*. Philadelphia: Fortress Press. Retrieved from http://religion-online.org

Ortlund, D., (2010). Power is made perfect in weakness (2 Cor 12:9): A biblical theology of strength through weakness. *Presbyterian, 36(2)*, 86-108.

Park, S., (2005). History and method of Charles V. Gerkin's pastoral theology: Toward an identity-embodied and community-embedded pastoral theology, Part 1.
    Pastoral Psychology, 54(1), 47-60.

Park, S. (2005). History and method of Charles V. Gerkin's

pastoral theology: Toward an identity-embodied and community-embedded pastoral theology, Part 2.
Pastoral Psychology, 54(1), 61-72.

Shay, J., (1995) *Achilles in Vietnam: Combat Trauma and the Undoing of Character*, Simon and Schuster.
Strauss, A. L., & Corbin, J. M., (1998). *Basics of qualitative research: Techniques and procedures for developing grounded theory.* Thousand Oaks: Sage Publications.

Tozer, A. W., & Zwemer, S. M., (1948). *The Pursuit of God.* Harrisburg, PA: Christian Publications.

Winter, D. G., (1998). The contributions of David McClelland to personality assessment.
Journal of Personality Assessment, 7(2), 129-145.

ACKNOWLEDGMENTS

First, I want to acknowledge God who makes all things possible. He was the inspiration and instigator for this project. He also led me to the many people who would eventually help me in this journey.

Next, I want to thank all the readers. There are two that stand out. First, Mr. Chuck Foster an engineer from JFHQ/MDW was there for the proof reading of the research paper and this book. He would often come into my office and scold me for not making adequate progress and shame me into working harder.

COL John Rosnow with the 335th SC (T)(P) spent hours patiently read all the chapters during the editing stage providing critical critiques to make sure that everything passed the sanity check.

Of course, my Mom was there reading every word at least one hundred times and sharing my excitement that this was really happening.

All the chaplains who shared their stories with me were invaluable to me. I won't ever forget them.

Douglas Glenn Clark was instrumental in helping me come up with the stories. This project would not have been possible without his creativity.

Sandi and Scott Tompkins edited the book. They took 100+ pages with some good ideas and carved it into a coherent story, while motivating me to get it published.

Finally, Shaun and Company for shining the flashlight navigating through the publishing process and for yanking me down the trail.

ABOUT THE AUTHOR

Chaplain (Lieutenant Colonel) Michael D. Jaques was born in Syracuse, NY and grew up in Pulaski, NY. He holds a BA in Political Science from Harding University, Searcy, AR. He holds a Masters of Divinity from The Southern Baptist Theological Seminary, Louisville, KY and a Doctor of Ministry from Louisville Presbyterian Theological Seminary.

Chaplain Michael D. Jaques is married with two children.

Copyright © 2020 by Michael D. Jaques LTC, US Army

All rights reserved.

No part of this book may be reproduced in any form or by any electronic or mechanical means, including information storage and retrieval systems, without written permission from the author, except for the use of brief quotations in a book review.

Made in the USA
Middletown, DE
01 June 2020

96397687R00080